Gay Ph

PROWLER PRESS Ltd.
Erotica from the sexperts!

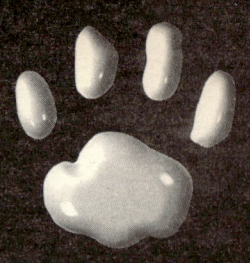

Get our free catalogue, filled with the very best gay-erotic magazines, videos, clothes, books & sex toys. Call the 24hr freephone:

☎ **0800 45 45 66**
+44 181 340 8644 *(international)*

Gay Phrase Book

**French German Spanish
Italian Dutch
Portuguese Japanese**

Barry McKay

FREEDOM EDITIONS

Dedication

To Angus

Acknowledgements

The author would like to thank the following people: Sijbout Colenbrander; Jack van der Wel (Homodok Centre, Amsterdam); Marcello Navas; Paulo Martins; Luiz Mott (Grupo Gay da Bahia, Brazil); Wladimir Padrós i Casalins; Carlos Aradas-Balbás; Juan Solis; Carlos (Mexico); Fernando Guasch; Filippo Giamblanco; Steffan Laas; Marc Staudacher; Jörg Schreiber; Michel Byrne; Suzanne Mitchell; Joanna Martinez; Manuel Montenegro; Tamaki Okamoto; Yoichi Takayama; Hiro Tsurunaga; Mako Nakai; Tobi Ringeling; Bert Neervoort; Claudio de Macedo; Carlos Bernat; Vittorio Circosta; Tony Howe; Keith Howes; Angus Donaldson; *Gay Scotland* (Edinburgh); Outright Scotland; Martin Walker; West & Wilde Bookshop (Edinburgh); Gay and Lesbian Switchboard, Amsterdam; Ian Withers (*OG*, Sydney); Brent Mackie (ACON, Sydney); Louise Jansen; Cedric Lee. Special thanks to Andriamparany who helped initiate the idea and write the guide. The safer sex dialogues were written by Sebastian Sandys of Gay Men Fighting AIDS (London). The Japanese safer sex dialogue was written by Arnel Landicho of the AIDS Council of New South Wales (ACON), Sydney, and Barry McKay.

Freedom Editions
an imprint of the Cassell Group
Wellington House
125 Strand
London WC2R 0BB

PO Box 605
Herndon
VA 20172

First published 1995. This edition 1997 © Barry McKay 1995, 1997.

All rights reserved. No part of this publication may be reproduced or transmitted in any form or by any means, electronic or mechanical including photocopying, recording or any information storage or retrieval system, without prior permission in writing from the publishers.

British Library Cataloguing-in-Publication Data
A catalogue record for this book is available from the British Library
ISBN: 0-304-33775-7 (paperback)

Designed and typeset by Ben Cracknell Studios

Printed in Great Britain by The Guernsey Press Co. Ltd

Contents

Notes on Symbols/Notes on Romanised Japanese   vi

French
- The Bar/Club — 1
- Cruising — 2
- At his place/your place — 7
- On the telephone — 10
- Health — 11
- Services — 11
- Contact ads — 12
- Expressions — 14
- Other useful vocabulary — 14
- Talking safer sex! — 18

German
- The Bar/Club — 20
- Cruising — 21
- At his place/your place — 25
- On the telephone — 29
- Health — 30
- Services — 30
- Contact ads — 31
- Expressions — 33
- Other useful vocabulary — 34
- Talking safer sex! — 37

Spanish
- The Bar/Club — 39
- Cruising — 40
- At his place/your place — 45
- On the telephone — 49
- Health — 49
- Services — 50
- Contact ads — 50
- Expressions — 53
- Other useful vocabulary — 53
- Talking safer sex! — 57

Italian
- The Bar/Club — 59
- Cruising — 60
- At his place/your place — 65
- On the telephone — 68
- Health — 69
- Services — 70
- Contact ads — 72
- Expressions — 73
- Other useful vocabulary — 73
- Talking safer sex! — 75

Dutch
- The Bar/Club — 77
- Cruising — 78
- At his place/your place — 83
- On the telephone — 86
- Health — 87
- Services — 87
- Contact ads — 88
- Expressions — 90
- Other useful vocabulary — 91
- Talking safer sex! — 94

Portuguese
- The Bar/Club — 96
- Cruising — 97
- At his place/your place — 102
- On the telephone — 105
- Health — 106
- Services — 106
- Contact ads — 107
- Expressions — 109
- Other useful vocabulary — 110
- Talking safer sex! — 113

Japanese
- The Bar/Club — 115
- Cruising — 116
- At his place/your place — 121
- On the telephone — 124
- Health — 124
- Services — 125
- Contact ads — 126
- Expressions — 129
- Other useful vocabulary — 130
- Talking safer sex! — 133

Notes on Symbols

- **;**   dividing entries when more than one translation or headword is available:

    a coffee   un café; un noir; un double (café)
    condoms; rubbers [UK]   des preservatifs; des capotes

- **/**   dividing alternatives within a translation:

    hot/cold milk   un lait chaud/froid
    with/without   avec…/sans…
    Are you on holiday [UK]/vacation [US]?   Es-tu en vacances (ici)?

- **( )**   denoting an optional word or phrase within a translation or headword:

    white coffee   un (café) crème; un café au lait
    (No thank you) I don't smoke   (Non merci) Je ne fume pas

- **[UK]**   denoting an English headword in British usage:

    a half-pint [UK]   un demi

- **[US]**   denoting an English headword in American usage:

    condoms; rubbers [US]   des preservatifs; des capotes

- **(adj)**   denoting an adjective:

    queer   gai *(adj)*; homo *(adj)*

- **(n)** neuter   **(m)** masculine
- **(f)** feminine   **(pl)** plural

Other symbols denote particular aspects of one of the languages used and are explained in the relevant section.

Notes on Romanised Japanese

A few helpful pointers about romanised Japanese: A long sounding vowel is written with a length sign over it e.g. 'ē' as in **remonēdo** lemonade which is pronounced like English lemonade. A long 'i' sound is written as 'ii'. Final 'u' is often pronounced weakly so it is hardly heard. This is specially so in words of foreign origin e.g. **orenji jūsu** orange juice or **kondōmu** condom, which both sound like their English equivalents. The sound 'su' is also very often pronounced weakly, so it sounds like 's'. e.g. How much is that? **ikura desuka** is pronounced as **ikura deska**?. In a similar manner, final 'o' in words of foreign origin are also often pronounced weakly to sound similar to their foreign equivalents e.g. **remonēdo** lemonade, or **sutorēto** straight. Japanese written 'r' is a sound which is pronounced similar to both English 'r' and 'l'.

'I' in Japanese: Both **watashi** and **boku** mean 'I' or 'me'. **watashi** can be used by both sexes, but **boku** by men only.

'You' in Japanese: In many cases, where it is obvious who you are talking to, the word for 'you' is omitted altogether. In informal circumstances, the word **kimi** can be used. In less informal situations **anata** can be used. Often, when talking to someone, in place of 'you' the person's name is used.

French

The Bar/Club – Le Bar/Le Club

I would like … please – Je voudrais … (s'il vous plaît)
- **a half-pint [UK]** – un demi
- **a pint [UK]** – un formidable; un sérieu
- **a beer** – une bière
- **a light beer** – une bière blonde; une blonde
- **a heavy beer [UK]** – une bière brune; une brune
- **a shandy [UK]** – un panaché
- **a glass of red wine** – un (vin) rouge; un (ballon de) rouge
- **a glass of white wine** – un (vin) blanc; un (ballon de) blanc
- **a vodka** – une vodka
- **a vodka and coke/orange** – une vodka coca/orange
- **a whisky; a scotch [US]** – un whisky
- **a rum** – un rhum
- **a cider** – un cidre
- **a coke** – un coca
- **a lemonade** – une limonade
- **an orange juice** – un jus d'orange
- **an apple juice** – un jus de pomme
- **a mineral water** – une eau minérale
- **a coffee** – un café; un noir; un double (café)
- **white coffee** – un (café) crème; un café au lait
- **a tea** – un thé
- **hot/cold milk** – un lait chaud/froid
- **a hot chocolate** – un chocolat chaud

with/without – avec…/sans…
- **sugar** – sucre
- **milk** – lait
- **ice** – glace
- **water** – eau
- **soda** – soda
- **tonic** – tonic
- **blackcurrant** – cassis
- **lemon juice** – jus de citron

How much is that? – C'est combien?; Combien je dois?; Ça coûte combien?

Is this seat free? – Est-ce que ce siège est libre?
- **Yes (it's free).** – Oui (c'est libre).
- **No (it's taken).** – Non (c'est pris).

Where are the toilets? – Où sont les toilettes?
- **at the back** – au fond

    on the right – à droite
    on the left – à gauche
    downstairs – en bas; au sous-sol
    upstairs – en haut; au premier (étage)

Do you sell anything to eat? – Avez-vous quelque chose à manger?; Servez-vous à manger?

something hot/cold – quelque chose de chaud/de froid

Have you got a menu? – Vous avez un menu?

Do you sell...? – Vendez-vous...?
    matches – des allumettes
    cigarettes – des cigarettes
    poppers – du poppers
    condoms; rubbers [US] – des préservatifs; des capotes
    lubricant – du lubrifiant

What time does this place close/open?
    – A quelle heure le bar ferme(-t-il)/ouvre(-t-il)?

At ... o'clock – À ... heure
    one – une
    two – deux
    three – trois
    four – quatre
    five – cinq
    six – six
    seven – sept
    eight – huit
    nine – neuf
    ten – dix
    eleven – onze
    twelve – douze
    half past one – une heure et demi

Cruising – Drague

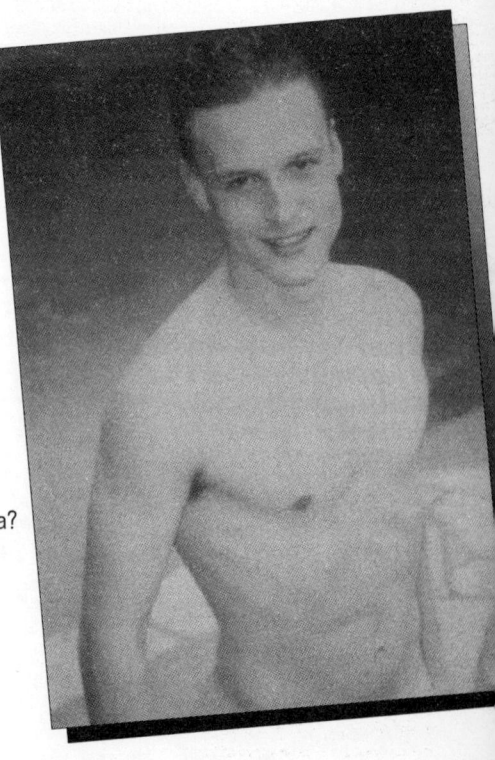

Hi! – Salut!

Hello! – Bonjour!

Good evening. – Bonsoir.

How are you? – (Comment) ça va?
    good – bien; oui, ça va
    OK – ça peut aller!

Do you speak...? – Parles-tu...?
    English – anglais
    French – français
    German – allemand
    Italian – italien
    Spanish – espagnol
    Dutch – hollandais
    Portuguese – portugais

Yes (I speak...). – Oui (je parle ...).
  a bit – un peu
No (I don't speak...). – Non (je ne parle pas...).
I'm sorry, I don't speak... – (Je suis) désolé, je ne parle pas...
I don't understand. – Je ne comprends pas.
Can you repeat that (please)? – Peux-tu répéter (s'il-te-plaît)? *(informal)*; Pouvez-vous répéter (s'il-vous-plaît)? *(formal)*
Can you speak more slowly please? – Peux-tu parler plus lentement (s'il-te plaît)? *(informal)*; Pouvez-vous parler plus lentement (s'il-vous-plaît)? *(formal)*
Have you got a light? – As-tu du feu?
Have you got the time? – As-tu l'heure?
Thank you! – Merci!
Are you on your own? – Es tu seul?
I'm with my boyfriend. – Je suis avec mon copain/mon mec/mon compagnon.
I'm with my friend/friends. – Je suis avec un ami. *(male friend)*; Je suis avec une amie. *(female friend)* /Je suis avec des amis.
What's your name? – Comment t'appelles-tu?
My name is... – Je m'appelle...
Where do you come from? – D'où viens-tu?
I come... – Je viens ...
  from **England** – d'Angleterre
  from **Scotland** – d'Ecosse
  from **Wales** – du Pays de Galles
  from **Britain** – de la Grande Bretagne
  from **Ireland** – de l'Irlande
  from **France** – de France
  from **Germany** – d'Allemagne
  from **Spain** – d'Espagne
  from **Portugal** – du Portugal
  from **Italy** – d'Italie
  from **Switzerland** – de Suisse
  from **Belgium** – de Belgique
  from **Austria** – d'Autriche
  from **Holland** – de Hollande; des Pays-Bas
  from **the United States** – des États-Unis
  from **Canada** – du Canada
  from **Japan** – du Japon
  from **Australia** – d'Australie
  from **New Zealand** – de la Nouvelle-Zélande
Do you come here often? – Viens-tu ici souvent?
Would you like ...? – Veux-tu...?
  a **drink** – un verre; un pot
  a **cigarette** – une cigarette
(No, thank you) I don't smoke. – (Non merci,) je ne fume pas.

Are you on holiday [UK]/vacation [US]? – Es-tu en vacances (ici)?
    Yes (I'm on holiday [UK]/vacation [US]). – Oui (Je suis en vacances).
    (No) I work here. – (Non) je travaille ici.
    I study here. – Je fais mes études ici; J'étudie ici.

Where do you live? – Où habites-tu?

Where are you staying? – Où habites-tu en ce moment?

I live... – J'habite...

I'm staying... – Je suis...
    with friends – chez des amis
    in a hotel – dans un hôtel
    in a flat [UK]/apartment [US] – dans un appartement
    in a house – dans une maison

Would you like to go...? – Veux-tu aller...?; Veux-tu qu'on aille...?
    to a cafe – dans un café
    to a restaurant – au restaurant
    to another bar – dans un autre bar
    to a disco – dans une disco
    to a sauna – au sauna
    to the beach – à la plage
    to the pool – à la piscine
    for a walk – faire un tour

Would you like to ... with me? – Veux-tu qu'on aille...?
    dance – danser
    have a drink – boire un verre; prendre un verre/un pot
    have something to eat – manger un morceau; manger ensemble

Can I buy you a drink? – Je peux t'offrir un verre?

What would you like (to drink)? – Qu'est-ce que tu veux (boire)?

It's ... here tonight, (isn't it?) – C'est ... ce soir ici, (n'est-ce pas)?
    packed – plein
    busy – animé
    dead – mort
    boring – chiant; emmerdant

I like ... – J'aime...
    your jacket – ta veste
    your shirt – ta chemise
    your clothes – ton look; tes fringues
    your haircut – ta coupe (de cheveux)

Where did you get it/them from? – Où l'as-tu eu (*or* eue)?/Où les as-tu eu(e)s?

Where did you get your hair done? – Qui t'a fait la coupe?

You look very smart/nice tonight! – Tu es très classe/n'es pas mal ce soir!

How old are you? – Quel âge as-tu?

I'm ... (years old). – J'ai ... ans.
(see numbers on page 16)

Nice eyes! – Quels beaux yeux (tu as)!

Nice legs! – Quelles jambes (tu as)!

At his place/your place – Chez lui/chez toi

Would you like some...? – Veux-tu...?
- coffee – du café
- tea – du thé
- wine – du vin
- orange juice – un jus d'orange

Would you like something to eat? – Veux-tu manger quelque chose?

Are you hungry/thirsty? – Tu as faim/soif?

Are you cold/too hot? – Tu as froid/trop chaud?

Do you want to watch TV/a video? – Veux-tu...

Would you like to listen to some music? – Ve...

What kind of music do you like? – Qu'est-ce q... genre de musique veux tu écouter?
- classical – de la musique classique
- opera – un opéra
- jazz – du jazz
- rock – du rock
- pop – du pop
- folk – du folk
- traditional – de la musique traditionnelle

Can I kiss you? – Je peux t'embrasser?

Would you like...? – Veux-tu ...?
- a massage – un massage
- a blow job – une pipe

What do you like doing? – Qu'est-que tu veux faire... aimes faire?

I like... – J'aime...

I don't like... – Je n'aime pas...

Do you like...? – Veux-tu...?; Aimes-tu...?
- kissing – embrasser
- cuddling – les câlins
- fucking – baiser; enculer
- being fucked – être baisé; être enculé
- sucking – tailler une pipe; sucer
- being sucked – être sucé
- wanking; jerking off [US] – branler; se branler(reciprocal); m...
- mutual masturbation – qu'on se branle
- licking – lécher
- stroking – caresser
- rubbing – frotter
- spanking – la fessée
- being spanked – avoir la fessée
- cross-dressing – me travestir (*Do you like...? Aimes-tu te trav...*)
- shaving – le rasage
- fisting – le fist fucking
- rimming – brouter

Nice bum! – Quel joli cul (tu as)!

What a nice smile you have! – Quel joli sourire (tu as)!

You're... – Tu es...
- beautiful – beau
- handsome – beau; pas mal
- hunky – bien foutu
- a hunk – un beau mec
- gorgeous – superbe
- sweet – doux; mignon
- cute – mignon
- sexy – sexy
- attractive – attirant; craquant; séduisant

You really turn me on. – Tu me fais craquer!; Tu m'excites!

You really make me hot. – Tu me mets le feu au cul!

I'm crazy about you. – Je suis accro!; Je suis mordu!

You're not my type. – Tu n'es pas mon genre.

I'm not interested. – Je ne suis pas intéressé.

Get lost! – Casse-toi!; Barre-toi!

Piss off! – Vas te faire foutre!; Vas te faire enculer!

What type of guys do you like? – Quel est le genre de mec qui te plaît?

What are you into? – Qu'est-ce que tu aimes?

I'm into... – J'aime...

I don't like... – Je n'aime pas...
- older men – les hommes plus agés
- younger men – les hommes plus jeunes
- blonde guys – les blonds
- guys with brown hair – les bruns
- guys with dark hair – les hommes aux cheveux noirs
- red heads – les roux
- guys with short hair – les hommes aux cheveux courts
- guys with long hair – les hommes aux cheveux longs
- hunky guys; well-built guys – les mecs bien foutus
- thin guys – les (mecs) minces
- chubby guys – les mecs enrobés
- tall guys – les grands (mecs)
- short guys – les petits (mecs)
- guys with dark eyes – les hommes aux yeux sombres
- guys with blue eyes – les hommes aux yeux bleus

What are you into? – Dans quoi es-tu?; Qu'est-ce qui t'intéresse?

I'm into... – Je suis dans...; Je suis intéressé par...

I'm not into...; I don't like... – Je ne suis pas dans...; Je ne suis pas intéressé par...; Je n'aime pas...
- denim – le jean
- leather – le cuir; la tenue de cuir
- rubber – le caoutchouc
- dildos – les godmichés

water sports – l'uro
fisting – le fist fucking
threesomes – les parties à trois (I don't like threeso...
cross-dressing – le travestisme
piercing – le perçage
tatoos – le tatouage
boots – les bottes
uniforms – les uniformes
brown; scat – le scato
bondage – le bondage

Is there somewhere quieter/more priva[te] – ...endroit plus tranquille/plus discret où on p[eut...]

Do you want to come to my place? – Veu[...]

Yes. – Oui.

I'm sorry, I can't. – (Je suis) désolé, je ne pe[ux...]

Can we meet again? – Peut-on se revoir?

When? – Quand?

Would you like to meet me... ? – Veux-tu qu[...]
  this evening – ce soir
  tomorrow – demain
  tomorrow morning – demain matin
  tomorrow afternoon – demain après-midi
  tomorrow night – demain soir
  on Monday – lundi
  on Tuesday – mardi
  on Wednesday – mercredi
  on Thursday – jeudi
  on Friday – vendredi
  on Saturday – samedi
  on Sunday – dimanche

At what time? – À quelle heure? *(see page 2)*

At ... o'clock – A ... heure

Where? – Où?
  here – ici
  at my hotel – à mon hôtel
  at my flat [UK]/apartment [US] – à mon appartemen[t]
  at my house – à ma maison
  at my friend's place – chez mon ami
  at your place – chez toi

Can I have your phone number? – Est-ce que [... ton] téléphone?

Can I have your address? – Est-ce que je [peux ...]

Bye. – Salut!

Goodbye. – Au revoir!

See you again! – À la prochaine!

Are you...?/I am ... – Est-tu ...?/Je suis...
  experienced – expert
  inexperienced – un bleu; sans expérience

I like to be... – Je préfère être...
  active – actif
  passive – passif

Shall we go to the bedroom/bathroom? – Peut-on aller dans la chambre/la salle de bain?

Have you got any...? – As-tu ...?
  condoms; rubbers [US] – des capotes; des préservatifs
  toys – des gadgets; des toys
  lubricant – du lubrifiant
  poppers – du poppers

Are you into safer sex? – Est-ce que tu es dans le "safer sex"/sexe à moindre risque?; Est-ce que tu pratiques le "safer sex"/sexe à moindre risque?

I'm only into safer sex. – J'aime seulement faire l'amour avec un préservatif; Je suis seulement dans le "safer sex"/sexe à moindre risque.

I'm HIV-positive. – Je suis séropositif.

Are you HIV-positive? – Es tu séropositif?

Would you like a shower (with me)? – Veux-tu prendre une douche (avec moi)?

Take off ...! – Enlève...!

Can I take off...? – (Est-ce que) je peux t'enlever...?
  your clothes – tes habits; tes fringues
  your shirt – ta chemise
  your trousers; your pants [US] – ton pantalon
  your socks – tes chaussettes
  your briefs; your underpants; your shorts [US] – ton slip; ton caleçon; ton short

Lie down! – Étends-toi!; Allonge-toi!

Bend over! – Courbe-toi!; Penche-toi!

Sit down! – Assieds-toi!; Assois-toi!

You're really nice. – Tu es (vraiment) chouette.

I like... – J'aime...

Can I kiss...? – (Est-ce que) je peux embrasser...?

Can I suck...? – (Est-ce que) je peux sucer...?

Can I touch...? – (Est-ce que) je peux toucher...?

Can I feel...? – (Est-ce que) je peux sentir...?
  your cock – ta queue; ta bite; ta verge; ta trique
  your balls – tes couilles
  your bum – ton cul
  your body – ton corps
  your figure – ton physique
  your nipples – les bouts des tes seins; tes tétons

your (hairy) chest – ton torse (velu/poilu)
your legs – tes jambes
your toe – ton doigt de pied; ton orteil

That feels good! – C'est bon!

That's great! – C'est super!; C'est le pied!

That's wonderful! – C'est extra!; C'est sensas!; C'est superbe!

That's really good! – C'est vraiment bon!

Do that again! – Encore!

My god, that's wonderful! – Bon dieu/Putain, c'est extra/sensas!

Yes...yes... – Oui...oui...

Come on! – Viens!

Fuck me! – Baise-moi!

Suck me! – Suce-moi!

Wank me! – Branle-moi!

Spank me! – Donne-moi la fessée!

Harder, harder! – Plus fort, plus fort!

Slower, slower! – Doucement, doucement!

I'm coming...! – Je viens...!; Je jouis...!

Come all over me! – Viens au-dessus de moi!

I don't like that! – Je n'aime pas ça!

Stop! – Arrête!; Stop!

That hurts! – Ça fait mal!

Not so fast/hard! – Pas si vite/fort!

Don't come in my mouth/arse! – Ne jouis pas dans ma bouche/mon cul!

That was wonderful. – C'était sensas.

Would you like to clean yourself up? – Veux-tu t'essuyer?

Have you got any tissues/ a towel? – As-tu des kleenex/une serviette?

Here you are! – Tiens!; Voilà!

May I use your shower? – Puis-je prendre une douche?

Shall we have a shower together? – Peux-t-on prendre une douche ensemble?

Can I have a towel (please)? – Est-ce que je peux avoir une serviette (s'il te plaît)?; Puis-je avoir une serviette (s'il te plaît)?

Good night! – Bonne nuit!

Sleep well! – Dors bien!

I love you. – Je t'aime (beaucoup).

Did you sleep well? – As-tu bien dormi?

I'll have to ask you to leave now – Maintenant je vais te demander de quitter.
Can you go now please? – Maintenant tu serais gentil de t'en aller.
I have to go now. – Il est temps que je m'en aille.
Would you like some breakfast? – Veux-tu (prendre) un petit déjeuner?
Can I write to you? – Est-ce que je peux t'écrire?
It's been nice knowing you! – Content de t'avoir connu/rencontré!
Would you like to see me again? – Tu veux qu'on se revoie?
Can I see you again? – Je peux te revoir?
Goodbye! – Salut!
See you again! – À la prochaine!; À bientôt!
Take care! – Prends soin de toi!; Porte-toi bien!

On the telephone – Au téléphone

Hello! – Allo!
Can I speak with ... (please)? – Est-ce que je peux parler à ... (s'il vous plaît)?
Hang on... – (Attendez) un moment...; Ne quittez pas...
...speaking! – C'est...!
It's me! – C'est moi!
It's... – C'est...
I'm phoning you as we arranged. – Je t'appelle comme convenu.
Can we meet ... – Peut-on se voir...
   this evening – ce soir
   at... o'clock – à ... heure (see page 2)
Where? – Où?
At... – À la...; Au...
Can you spell it? – Peux-tu épeler (s'il te plaît)?(*informal*); Pouvez-vous épeler (s'il vous plaît)?(*formal*)
OK, thank you! – OK, merci!
See you later! – À plus tard!
He is not here! – Il n'est pas là!
Can you phone again... – Rappelez (de nouveau) ...
   later – plus tard
   this afternoon – cet après-midi
I don't understand. – Je ne comprends pas!
Do you speak...? – Parlez-vous...?(*formal*);Parles-tu...?(*informal*)
Please speak slowly. – Parlez lentement s'il vous plaît. (*formal*); Parle lentement s'il te plaît. (*informal*)

Health – Santé

I need to see a doctor. – Il me faut un médecin.
doctor – le docteur; le médecin
surgery [UK]; doctor's office [US] – le cabinet (du médecin)
chemist [UK]; pharmacy – la pharmacie
I have... – J'ai...
I have caught... – J'ai attrapé...
I think I have... – Je crois que j'ai...
Do you have something for...? – Avez-vous quelque chose contre...?
  gonorrhoea – la chaude-pisse; la blennorragie
  syphilis – la syphilis
  crabs – les morpions *(with 'I have..')* ; des morpions *(with 'Do you have something for...?')*
  lice – des poux *(with 'I have..')* ; les poux *(with 'Do you have something for...?')*
  herpes – l'herpès
  scabies – la gale
I hurt here. – J'ai mal ici.
I'm bleeding. – Je saigne.
I'm itching. – J'ai des démangeaisons.
My throat/penis/anus hurts. – J'ai mal à la gorge/au pénis/au derrière.

Services – Services

Can you help me? – Pouvez-vous m'aider (s'il vous-plaît)? *(formal)*; Peux-tu m'aider (s'il-te-plaît)? *(informal)*
How much is this/that? – Ça coûte combien? C'est combien?
Have you got a map of...? – Avez-vous un plan de...?
the city – la ville
Can I have the number for Gay Switchboard? – Puis-je avoir le numéro des renseignements téléphoniques homos/gais?
Can I have the number of the AIDS helpline? – Puis-je avoir le numéro (de téléphone) du SIDA info service?
Can you give me the name of a doctor who is experienced in AIDS/HIV-related problems? – Pouvez vous me donner le nom d'un médecin compétent en matière du VIH/du SIDA?
Can you give me the name of a clinic which is experienced in AIDS/HIV-related problems? – Pouvez vous me donner le nom d'un hôpital compétent en matière du VIH/du SIDA?
Can you give me the name of a gay-friendly doctor? – Pouvez-vous me recommander un docteur sympa avec les gais?
Excuse me! – Excusez-moi!

Where is/are...? – Où se trouve...?/Où se trouvent...?
- **the sauna** – le sauna
- **the cruising areas** – les lieux de drague
- **the gay bars** – les bars homos/gais
- **the cottages [UK]; tea rooms [US]** – les tasses
- **the gay bookshop** – la librairie gaie
- **the gay hotels** – les hôtels gais

Contact ads – Les petites annonces

I am... – Je suis...

I am looking for a...guy – Je cherche/recherche un mec...
- **active** – actif
- **affectionate** – affectueux; plein de tendresse; tendre
- **athletic** – athlétique; musclé
- **attractive** – attirant; craquant
- **bisexual** – bissexuel
- **boyish** – gamin; enfantin
- **caring** – prévenant
- **Christian** – chrétien
- **chubby** – enrobé
- **clean** – soigné; avec bonne présentation; J'ai une bonne présentation *(I am clean)*
- **clean-shaven** – rasé de près
- **conservative** – conservateur
- **considerate** – attentionné
- **cuddly** – câlin; caressant; doux
- **cute** – mignon
- **discreet** – discret
- **dominant** – dominateur
- **easy-going** – accommodant; facile à vivre; décontracté; communicatif
- **educated** – cultivé; avec bonne éducation; J'ai une bonne éducation *(I am educated)*
- **experienced** – expert
- **friendly** – sympa
- **gentle** – gentil; doux
- **good-looking** – pas mal; bien; joli
- **hairy** – poilu; velu
- **handsome** – beau; pas mal
- **honest** – honnête; intègre
- **horny** – excité; ardent; sensuel
- **with a good sense of humour** – avec sens de l'humour; J'ai le sens de l'humour *(I have a good sense of humour);* marrant; drôle; plein d'humour
- **independent** – indépendant
- **inexperienced** – novice
- **intelligent** – intelligent
- **interesting** – intéressant
- **introverted** – introverti
- **lonely** – solitaire
- **loyal** – loyal; fidèle
- **married** – marié
- **masculine** – viril; masculin
- **mature** – mature
- **of medium build** – de corpulence moyenne
- **middle aged** – d'un certain âge; entre deux âges

military – militaire; mec en treillis
muscular – musclé
a nature lover – un ami de la nature; aimant la nature
non-scene – hors milieu; hors ghetto
a non-smoker – un non-fumeur
older – plus vieux
open – ouvert; franc; pas coincé
open minded – libéral; large d'esprit; ouvert d'esprit
outgoing – extraverti
passionate – passionné
passive – passif
quiet – calme
radical – radical
refined – cultivé
reliable – sérieux; de confiance; sûr
reserved – réservé
romantic – romantique
of the same age – du même âge
sensitive – sensible
serious – sérieux; sincère; vrai; droit
shy – timide; pudique
sincere – sincère
slim – mince; svelte
a smoker – un fumeur
smooth – imberbe
special – particulier; singulier; special
spontaneous – spontané
sporty – sportif
straight acting – au look hétéro; naturel; hétérolooké
straight forward – franc
a student – (un) étudiant
submissive – docile; soumis
tall – grand
transsexual – transsexuel
a university graduate – de formation universitaire
virgin – puceau; vierge
warm – chaleureux
well-endowed; well-hung – bien monté; TBM *(meaning 'très bien monté')*
well-built – bien bâti; costaud; baraqué; robuste
young – jeune
younger – plus jeune
youthful – jeune; au look jeune; J'ai un look jeune *(I am boyish)*

no effeminates – efféminés s'absteni; non efféminés

no fats – gros s'abstenir; non gros

...welcome – ...bienvenu (-s *if plural*)

for friendship – pour amitié

for a relationship – pour (une) relation amicale

for sex – pour bonne baise

...only – seulement...

I have... – J'ai...

blue eyes – les yeux bleus
brown eyes – les yeux marrons
green eyes – les yeux verts
grey eyes – les yeux gris/noisettes
blonde hair – les cheveux blonds; Je suis blond
 (I am blonde)
brown hair – les cheveux châtains; Je suis châtain
 (I have brown hair)
black hair – les cheveux noirs
red hair – les cheveux roux; Je suis roux
 (I have red hair)
grey hair – les cheveux poivre et sel
dark hair – les cheveux bruns; Je suis brun
 (I have dark hair)
short hair – les cheveux courts
long hair – les cheveux longs

I have a beard. – Je suis barbu.

I have a moustache. – Je suis moustachu.

I'm bald. – Je suis chauve.

Expressions – Expressions

My God! – Putain!; Bon dieu!

Fantastic! – Fantastique!; Sensas!; Fabuleux!

I'm sorry. – (Je suis) désolé.

Excuse me! – Excuse-moi! *(informal)*; Excusez-moi! *(formal)*; Pardon!

Get fucked! – Vas te faire foutre!; Vas te faire enculer!

Fuck off! – Casse-toi!; Barre-toi!; Dégage!

Shit! – Merde!

Darling! – Mon chéri!; Mon amour!; Mon chou!

My dear! – Mon chéri!; Mon amour!

Honey! – (Mon) trésor!; Mon chou!

Oh dear! – Mon dieu!; Bon dieu!; Putain!; Merde!

How wonderful! – (C'est) merveilleux!; (C'est) extra!; (C'est) sensas!

How awful! – C'est dégueulasse!; C'est affreux!

He's a friend of Dorothy. – Il en est; C'en est une.

As camp as knickers. – C'est une complète/véritable folle; Elle est complètement folle; Elle est délirante.

Wow! – Quel délire!

Other useful vocabulary – Vocabulaire complémentaire

Yes. – Oui.

No. – Non.

I am... – je suis...

he is... – il est...

you are... – tu es... *(informal)*; vous êtes... *(formal)*

my friend is... – mon ami est...*(male friend)*; mon amie est...*(female friend)*

my friends are... – mes amis sont... *(male friends)* ; mes amises sont...*(female friends) (adj + (e)s)*

my boyfriend is... – mon copain/mec est...

adult – adulte

AIDS – le SIDA

bent [UK]; homo [US] – pédé *(adj)*

bisexual – bissexuel *(both adj. and noun)*; à voile et à vapeur

a bitch – une garce; une salope; un salaud

to bitch – être vache; dire des vacheries (sur quelqu'un)

bitchy – vache; salope

body-building – le culturisme; le culto; faire de la culture physique

butch – macho

camp – camp; folle *(very camp)*

to chat someone up – baratiner quelqu'un

to be 'in the closet' – être planqué; se planquer; non avoué; au placard

come; spunk – le foutre; le jus

to come – venir; jouir; éjaculer; juter

to 'come out' – s'afficher/se déclarer (ouvertement) gai; sortir du placard

a cow – une vache; un chameau; une conne

to cruise – draguer

drag – travesti; en travesti; le travelo

drag shows – des spectacles de travesti

a dyke [UK]; a lesbo [US] – une gouine; une goudou; une gousse

a butch dyke – une gouine hommasse; une garçonne

erect – bandé

an erection; a hard-on – une érection; avoir la trique *(to have a hard-on)*; bander dur *(to have a hard-on)*

a fag hag – une soeurette; une fille à pédé

female – féminin; femme *(noun)*

french-kissing – un patin; rouler un patin *(verb)*

a fuck – une baise; une bourre

gay – le gai; l' homo; le pédé *(nouns)*; gai; homo; pédé *(adjectives)*

the gay scene – le milieu gai; le ghetto
a girl – une nana
a guy – un mec; un garçon
the leather scene – le milieu cuir
a lesbian – une lesbienne
male – masculin; homme *(noun)*
men only – hommes exclusivement; seulement pour hommes
the nightclub – le nightclub
the nudist beach – la plage nudiste
to pick someone up – lever quelqu'un
to be pissed off with someone – en avoir marre de quelqu'un
a poof; a faggot [US] – une tante; une tapette; une tantouse
a queen – une folle; une tante; une pédale; une tapette; une tata
queer – gai; homo*(adjectives)*
queer-bashing – la chasse aux pédés
a rent-boy – un garçon de passe; un truqueur
SM (sadomasochism) – le sadomasochisme
skinheads – les skinheads
a slut – une salope; une putain
straight – hétéro
a tart – une poule; une grue; une salope; une pute; une putain
a transvestite – un travesti
a wank – une branlette
women only – femmes exclusivement; seulement pour femmes

one – un (m); une (f)	**twelve** – douze	**thirty** – trente
two – deux	**thirteen** – treize	**forty** – quarante
three – trois	**fourteen** – quatorze	**fifty** – cinquante
four – quatre	**fifteen** – quinze	**sixty** – soixante
five – cinq	**sixteen** – seize	**seventy** – soixante-dix
six – six	**seventeen** – dix-sept	**eighty** – quatre-vingts
seven – sept	**eighteen** – dix-huit	**ninety** – quatre-vingt-dix
eight – huit	**nineteen** – dix-neuf	**one hundred** – cent
nine – neuf	**twenty** – vingt	**one thousand** – mille
ten – dix	**twenty one** – vingt-et-un	
eleven – onze	**twenty two** – vingt-deux	

Talking safer sex!

On the train – Dans le train

Excuse me, is this seat taken?
Pardon, cette place est prise?

No, I don't think so.
Non, je ne pense pas.

> **(Many furtive glances later...**
> *Après bien des regards furtifs...)*

Do you have the time?
Vous avez l'heure?

Four thirty.
Quatre heures et demi.

> **(Later...**
> *Un moment passe...)*

This train is quiet.
Ce train est bien calme.

Yes, we seem to have this carriage to ourselves.
C'est vrai, on a le compartiment à nous seuls.

Where are you going?
Vous allez où?

Venice.
A Venise.

Oh, are you on your own?
Ah bon.....et vous voyagez seul?

I'm meeting my boyfriend there in a couple of days.
Mon ami doit me rejoindre. Il arrivera dans quelques jours.

> **(Noticing carefully placed hand gently stroking crotch...**
> *Sa main travaille gentiment entre ses cuisses - ça ne passe pas inaperçu...)*

Do you mind if I sit here? I don't like travelling backwards.
Ça te gênerait que je m'assieds à côté de toi? Je n'aime pas voyager le dos à la marche du train.

No, not at all.
Non, non, je t'en prie.

> **(Train enters tunnel...**
> *Le train entre dans un tunnel...)*

Mmmm, that was good, somebody knows how to kiss!
Mmmm, c'était bon. En voilà un qui sait embrasser!

I've had lots of practice.
Je ne manque pas de pratique.

What else have you been practicing?
Et tu pratiques quoi encore?

My blow jobs could win prizes.
Mon coup de pipe est assez réputé.

Show me!
Fais voir un peu!

Oh God, that's good! Lick my balls - oooh!
Putain, que c'est bon! Vas-y, lèche-moi les couilles - oooh!

That's good. I'd love to fuck you!
Comme c'est bon!… J'aimerais vraiment te baiser!

Do you think it's safe to do it here?
Ce n'est pas un peu risqué ici?

Yeah, go on, I've got a bag full of condoms here.
Mais non, j'ai des capotes plein les poches.

OK...
Alors dans ce cas…

That feels really good!
Que c'est bon!

Oh yeah!
Oh oui!

Shit, somebody's coming!
Merde, voilà quelqu'un!

(Enter very cute ticket collector...
Un contrôleur beau mec fait son entrée…)

• Don't mind me, boys. Now I hope one of you hasn't got a ticket! There are lots of ways to pay your train fare!
• Ne vous gênez pas pour moi, messieurs! J'espère que l'un de vous a égaré son billet - il y a bien des façons de les payer, les amendes!

That's funny, I think I've lost my ticket. What did you have in mind?
Justement, c'est bizarre, je ne le trouve pas, mon billet.
Vous pouvez me suggérer quelque chose?

• Well, you just carry on with what you're doing.
• Pourquoi pas continuer la partie?

OK, why don't you join in?
OK, vous pourriez peut-être nous filer un coup de main?

• Sounds good to me...
• Je ne dirais pas non.

German

The Bar/Club – Die Kneipe/Der Klub

I would like... please – Kann ich...haben, bitte?; ..., bitte.
- **a half-pint [UK]** – ein kleines Bier
- **a pint [UK]** – ein großes Bier
- **a beer** – ein Bier
- **a light beer** – ein helles Bier
- **a heavy beer [UK]** – ein Altbier; ein dunkles Bier
- **a shandy [UK]** – einen Radler; ein Alster
- **a glass of red wine** – ein Glas Rotwein
- **a glass of white wine** – ein Glas Weißwein
- **a gin and tonic** – einen Gin-Tonic
- **a vodka** – einen Wodka
- **a vodka and coke/orange** – einen Cola-Wodka/Orange-Wodka
- **a whisky; a scotch [US]** – einen Whisky
- **a rum** – einen Rum
- **a cider** – einen Apfelwein
- **a coke** – eine Cola
- **a lemonade** – eine Limonade; eine Sprite
- **an orange juice** – einen O-Saft; einen Orangensaft
- **an apple juice** – einen Apfelsaft
- **a mineral water** – ein Mineralwasser
- **a coffee** – einen Kaffee
- **white coffee** – Kaffee mit Milch
- **a tea** – einen Tee
- **hot/cold milk** – ein Glas warme/kalte Milch
- **a hot chocolate** – eine heiße Schokolade

with/without – mit.../ohne...
- **sugar** – Zucker
- **milk** – Milch
- **ice** – Eis
- **water** – Wasser
- **soda** – Soda
- **tonic** – Tonic
- **blackcurrant** – schwarzem Johannisbeersaft
- **lemon juice** – Zitronensaft

How much is that? – Was kostet das?

Is this seat free? – Ist hier frei?
- **Yes (it's free).** – Ja (hier ist frei).
- **No (it's taken).** – Nein (es ist besetzt).

Where are the toilets? – Wo sind die Toiletten?
- **at the back** – ganz hinten
- **on the right** – rechts
- **on the left** – links

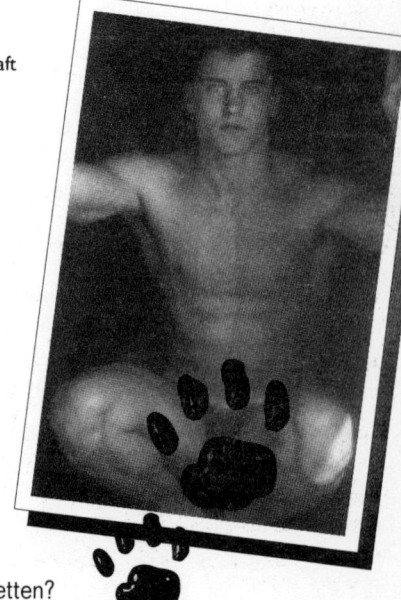

downstairs – unten
upstairs – oben

Do you sell anything to eat? – Gibt es hier etwas zu Essen?

something hot/cold – etwas warmes/kaltes

Have you got a menu? – Haben Sie eine Speisekarte?

Do you sell...? – Habt ihr ...?
   matches – Streichhölzer
   cigarettes – Zigaretten
   poppers – Poppers
   condoms; rubbers [US] – Kondome; Pariser; Präservative; Gummis
   lubricant – Gleitmittel; Gleitcreme

What time does this place close/open? – Wann macht Ihr zu/auf?

At ...o'clock – Um...
   one – eins
   two – zwei
   three – drei
   four – vier
   five – fünf
   six – sechs
   seven – sieben
   eight – acht
   nine – neun
   ten – zehn
   eleven – elf
   twelve – zwölf
   half past one – halb zwei *(in German: half of the following hour)*

Cruising – Cruisen

Hi! – Hi!; Hallo!

Hello! – Guten Tag!; Grüß Gott!

Good evening. – Guten Abend.

How are you? – Wie geht's?
   good – gut
   OK – OK

Do you speak... – Sprichst Du...?
   English – Englisch
   French – Französisch
   German – Deutsch
   Italian – Italienisch
   Spanish – Spanisch
   Dutch – Holländisch
   Portuguese – Portugiesisch

Yes (I speak...). – Ja (ich spreche...).
   a bit – ein bißchen

No (I don't speak...). – Nein (ich kann kein...sprechen).

I'm sorry, I don't speak ... – Es tut mir leid, ich kann kein...

I don't understand. – Ich verstehe Dich nicht. *(informal)*; Ich verstehe Sie nicht. *(formal)*

Can you repeat that (please)? – Kannst Du das bitte wiederholen? *(informal)*; Können Sie das bitte wiederholen? *(formal)*

Can you speak more slowly please? – Kannst Du etwas langsamer sprechen, bitte? *(informal)*; Können Sie etwas langsamer sprechen, bitte? *(formal)*

Have you got a light? – Hast Du Feuer?

Have you got the time? – Wie spät ist es?

Thank you! – Danke!

Are you on your own? – Bist du alleine?

I'm with my boyfriend. – Ich bin hier mit meinem Freund.

I'm with a friend/friends. – Ich bin hier mit einem Freund/Freunden.

What's your name? – Wie heißt Du?

My name is... – Ich heiße...

Where do you come from? – Woher kommst Du?

I come from... – Ich komme aus...
  England – England
  Scotland – Schottland
  Wales – Wales
  Britain – Großbritannien
  Ireland – Irland
  France – Frankreich
  Germany – Deutschland
  Spain – Spanien
  Portugal – Portugal
  Italy – Italien
  Switzerland – der Schweiz
  Belgium – Belgien
  Austria – Österreich
  Holland – Holland
  the United States – Amerika; den USA
  Canada – Kanada
  Japan – Japan
  Australia – Australien
  New Zealand – Neuseeland

Do you come here often? – Bist Du oft hier?

Would you like ...? – Möchtest Du...?; Willst Du...?
  a drink – etwas trinken
  a cigarette – eine Zigarette

(No, thank you) I don't smoke. – (Nein danke,) ich rauche nicht.

Are you on holiday [UK]/vacation [US]? – Machst Du hier Urlaub?
  Yes (I'm on holiday [UK]/vacation [US]) – Ja (ich mache Urlaub)
  (No) I work here. – (Nein) ich arbeite hier.
  I study here. – Ich studiere hier.

Where do you live? – Wo wohnst Du?

Where are you staying? – Wo übernachtest Du?

I live... – Ich wohne...

I'm staying... – Ich übernachte...
    with friends – bei Freunden
    in a hotel – in einem Hotel
    in a flat [UK]/apartment [US] – in einer Wohnung
    in a house – in einem Haus

Would you like to go ...? – Sollen wir...gehen?
    to a cafe – in ein Café
    to a restaurant – in ein Restaurant
    to another bar – in eine andere Bar/Kneipe
    to a disco – in eine Diskothek
    to a sauna – in eine Sauna
    to the beach – an den Strand
    to the pool – in ein Schwimmbad; zum Swimmingpool
    for a walk – spazieren

Would you like to ... with me? – Wollen wir...?
    dance – tanzen
    have a drink – etwas trinken
    have something to eat – etwas essen gehen

Can I buy you a drink? – Kann ich Dir etwas zu trinken bestellen?

What would you like (to drink)? – Was möchtest Du trinken?

It's ... here tonight, (isn't it?) – Es ist ... hier heute abend, (nicht?/oder?)
    packed – gerammelt voll
    busy – ziemlich voll
    dead – ziemlich tot
    boring – (ziemlich) langweilig

I like your ... – Ich mag...; ...gefällt mir.
    jacket – deine Jacke
    shirt – dein Hemd
    clothes – deine Klamotten; deine Kleidung; deine Sachen
    haircut – deine Haare; deinen Haarschnitt

Where did you get it/them from? – Wo hast Du die/das (for 'Hemd') her?

Where did you get your hair done? – Wo läßt Du deine Haare schneiden?

You look very smart/nice tonight! – Du siehst heute abend aber toll/gut aus!

How old are you? – Wie alt bist Du?

I'm... (years old) – Ich bin...
(see numbers on page 36)

Nice eyes! – Schöne Augen!

Nice legs! – Schöne Beine!

Nice bum! – Geiler Arsch!; Schöner Hintern!

What a nice smile you have! – Ich mag dein Lächeln.

You're... – Du bist...

beautiful – schön
handsome – gutaussehend
hunky – gut gewachsen; Du bist aber tierisch *(you're hunky)*; Du hast eine geile Figur *(you're hunky)*
a hunk – gut gebaut
gorgeous – geil; hinreißend
sweet – lieb; süss
cute – hübsch
sexy – sexy; aufreizend
attractive – attraktiv

You really turn me on. – Du machst mich an!; Ich bin geil auf Dich!

You really make me hot. – Du machst mich heiß!

I'm crazy about you. – Ich bin verrückt auf Dich!

You're not my type. – Du bist nicht mein Typ.

I'm not interested. – Ich bin nicht interessiert.

Get lost! – Verschwinde!

Piss off! – Hau ab!; Verpiß dich!

What type of guys do you like? – Was magst Du so für Typen?

What are you into? – Worauf stehst Du?

I'm into... – Ich stehe auf...; Ich mag...

I'm not into...; I don't like... – Ich stehe nicht auf...

older men – ältere Männer
younger men – jüngere Männer
blonde guys – Blonde; blonde Männer
guys with brown hair – Männer mit braunem Haar
guys with dark hair – dunkelhaarige Männer; Männer mit dunklem Haar
red heads – Rothaarige; rothaarige Männer; Männer mit rotem Haar
guys with short hair – Kurzhaarige; kurzhaarige Männer; Männer mit kurzem Haar
guys with long hair – Langhaarige; langhaarige Männer; Männer mit langem Haar
hunky guys; well-built guys – gut gebaute Männer
thin guys – schlanke Männer
chubby guys – mollige Männer
tall guys – große Männer
short guys – kleine Männer
guys with dark eyes – Männer mit dunklen Augen
guys with blue eyes – Männer mit blauen Augen
denim – Jeans
leather – Leder
rubber – Gummi
dildos – Dildos
water sports – Natursekt; Pißspiele; anpissen
fisting – Fistfucking; Faustficken; Fisten
threesomes – Dreier
cross-dressing – Frauenkleidung
piercing – Körperschmuck; Intimschmuck; Piercing
tatoos – Tatoos; Tätowierungen
boots – Springerstiefel; Rangerstiefel; Armeestiefel
uniforms – Uniformen
brown; scat – Braun; Scat; Dirty *(includes 'water sports'!)*
bondage – Bondage; Fesseln

Is there somewhere quieter/more private we can go? – Können wir irgendwo hingehen, wo es etwas ruhiger ist?
Do you want to come to my place? – Sollen wir zu mir gehen?
Yes. – Ja.
I'm sorry, I can't. – Es tut mir leid, ich kann nicht.
Can we meet again? – Können wir uns wiedersehen?
When? – Wann?
Would you like to meet me...? – Hast Du Lust, mich ... zu treffen?
   this evening – heute abend
   tomorrow – morgen
   tomorrow morning – morgen früh
   tomorrow afternoon – morgen nachmittag
   tomorrow night – morgen Abend
   on Monday – am Montag
   on Tuesday – am Dienstag
   on Wednesday – am Mittwoch
   on Thursday – am Donnerstag
   on Friday – am Freitag
   on Saturday – am Samstag
   on Sunday – am Sonntag
At what time? – Um wieviel Uhr?
At ... o'clock – Um...Uhr *(see page 21)*
Where? – Wo?
   here – hier
   at my hotel – in meinem Hotel
   at my flat [UK]/apartment [US] – bei mir; in meiner Wohnung
   at my house – bei mir; in meinem Haus
   at my friend's place – bei meinem Freund
   at your place – bei Dir
Can I have your phone number? – Kann ich Deine Telefonnummer haben?
Can I have your address? – Kann ich Deine Addresse haben?
Bye. – Tschüß!; Tschau!
Goodbye. – Auf Wiedersehen!
See you again! – Bis bald!

At his place/your place – Bei ihm/bei Dir

Would you like some...? – Möchtest Du...?
   coffee – Kaffee
   tea – Tee
   wine – Wein
   orange juice – Orangensaft
Would you like something to eat? – Möchtest Du etwas essen?
Are you hungry/thirsty? – Hast Du Hunger/Durst?

Are you cold/too hot? – Ist Dir kalt?/Ist es Dir zu warm?

Do you want to watch TV/a video? – Möchtest Du fernsehen/ein Video sehen?

Would you like to listen to some music? – Möchtest Du Musik hören?

What kind of music do you like? – Was für Musik magst Du?
  classical – klassische Musik
  opera – Oper
  jazz – Jazz
  rock – Rock
  pop – Pop
  folk – Folk
  traditional – Volkslieder

Can I kiss you? – Kann ich Dich einen Kuß geben?

Would you like...? – Möchtest Du...?
  a massage – eine Massage
  a blow job – einen geblasen bekommen

What do you like doing? – Worauf stehst Du?

I like... – Ich stehe auf...; Ich mag...

I don't like... – Ich stehe nicht auf...; Ich mag... nicht.

Do you like...? – Stehst Du auf...?; Magst Du...?
  kissing – küssen
  cuddling – schmusen; kuscheln
  fucking – bumsen; ficken
  sucking – blasen; lecken
  wanking; jerking off [US] – wichsen
  mutual masturbation – daß wir uns zusammen einen runterholen (*only use with* 'Ich mag...'; 'Ich mag... nicht' *or* 'Magst Du...?')
  licking – lecken
  stroking – streicheln
  rubbing – reiben
  cross-dressing – Frauenkleidung
  shaving – rasieren; Rasur
  fisting – Fistfucking; Faustficken; Fisten
  rimming – Arschlecken; Rimming

I like... – Ich stehe darauf...

I don't like... – Ich stehe nicht darauf...

Do you like...? – Stehst Du darauf...?
  being fucked – gebumst zu werden; gefickt zu werden
  being sucked – einen geblasen zu bekommen

I like... – Ich möchte Dir einen...

I don't like... – Ich möchte Dir keinen ....

Do you like...? – Möchtest Du mir einen...?
  spanking – Klapps auf den Arsch geben

I like... – Ich möchte einen...

I don't like... – Ich möchte mir keinen...

Do you like...? – Möchtest Du einen...?
  being spanked – Klapps auf den Arsch bekommen

Are you...?/I am ... – Bist Du...?/ Ich bin...
  experienced – erfahren
  inexperienced – unerfahren

I like to be... – Ich bin lieber...
  active – aktiv
  passive – passiv

Shall we go to the bedroom/bathroom? – Sollen wir ins Schlafzimmer/ ins Bad gehen?

Have you got any...? – Hast Du...?
  condoms; rubbers [US] – Kondome; Pariser; Präservative; Gummis
  toys – Toys
  lubricant – Gleitmittel; Gleitcreme
  poppers – Poppers

Are you into safer sex? – Machst Du Safer Sex?

I'm only into safer sex. – Ich mache nur Safer Sex.

I'm HIV-positive. – Ich bin HIV-positiv.

Are you HIV-positive? – Bist Du HIV-positiv?

Would you like a shower (with me)? – Willst Du (mit mir) duschen?

Take off...! – Ziehe ... aus!

Can I take off...? – Kann ich Dir ... ausziehen?
  your clothes – Deine Sachen
  your shirt – Dein Hemd
  your trousers; your pants [US] – Deine Hosen
  your socks – Deine Socken
  your briefs; your underpants; your shorts [US] – Dein Slip; Deine Unterhosen; Deine Shorts

Lie down! – Leg Dich hin!

Bend over! – Beug Dich über!; Bück Dich!

Sit down! – Setz Dich!

You're really nice – Ich mag Dich wirklich gern!

I like ... – Ich mag...

Can I kiss...? – Kann ich...küssen?

Can I suck...? – Kann ich...blasen?

Can I touch...? – Kann ich...anfassen?

Can I feel...? – Kann ich...berühren?
  your cock – Deinen Schwanz; Dein Ding; Deine Rute; Deine Latte
  your balls – Deine Eier
  your bum – Deinen Hintern; Deinen Arsch
  your body – Deinen Körper
  your figure – Deine Figur
  your nipples – Deine Brustwarzen; Deine Nippel

your (hairy) chest – Deine (haarige) Brust
your legs – Deine Beine
your toe – Deine Zehe

That feels good! – Das tut gut!
That's great! – (Das ist) stark!
That's wonderful! – (Das ist) toll!
That's really good! – (Das ist) irre!; (das ist) geil!
Do that again! – Noch mal!
My god, that's wonderful! – Das ist so geil!
Yes...yes... – Ja...ja...
Come on...! – Los....!
Fuck me! – Fick mich!
Suck me! – Blas mir einen!
Wank me! – Hol mir einen runter!; Wichs mich!
Spank me! – Schlag mich!
Harder, harder! – Mehr!,mehr!; Doller!,doller!
Slower, slower! – Langsamer, langsamer!
I'm coming...! – Ich komme...!; Mir kommts...!

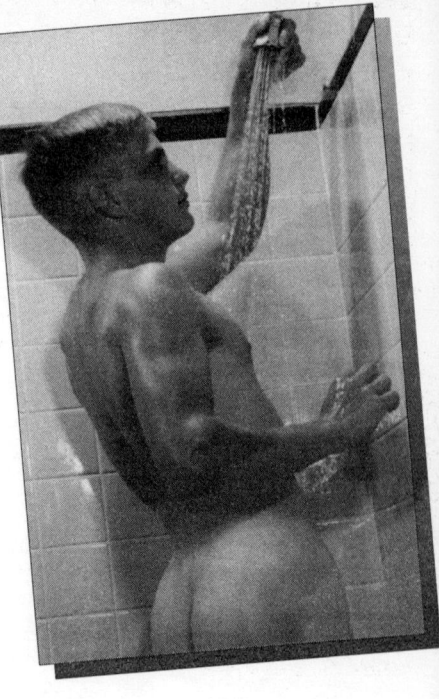

Come all over me! – Komm auf mir!
I don't like that! – Ich mag das nicht!
Stop! – Stop!; Hör auf!
That hurts! – Das tut weh!
Not so fast/hard! – Nicht so schnell/stark!
Don't come in my mouth/arse! – Bitte komme nicht in meinem Mund/Arsch (or) Hintern!
That was wonderful. – Das war wunderbar.
Would you like to clean yourself up? – Möchtest Du Taschentücher haben?; Möchtest Du ins Bad? *(meaning: 'Would you like to use the bathroom?')*
Have you got any tissues/ a towel? – Hast Du Taschentücher/ein Handtuch?
Here you are! – Da!; Hier!
May I use your shower? – Kann ich duschen?

Shall we have a shower together? – Wollen wir zusammen duschen?
Can I have a towel (please)? – Hast Du ein Handtuch für mich?
Good night! – Gute Nacht!
Sleep well! – Schlaf gut!; Schlaf schön!
I love you. – Ich liebe Dich.
Did you sleep well? – Hast Du gut geschlafen?
I'll have to ask you to leave now. – Ich muß Dich leider bitten, jetzt zu gehen.
Can you go now please? – Kannst Du jetzt bitte gehen?
I have to go now. – Also, ich muß jetzt gehen.
Would you like some breakfast? – Willst Du etwas zum Frühstück?
Can I write to you? – Kann ich Dir schreiben?
It's been nice knowing you! – Es war schön mit Dir!
Would you like to see me again? – Möchtest Du mich wiedersehen?
Can I see you again? – Kann ich Dich wiedersehen?
Goodbye! – Tschüß!
See you again! – Bis bald!
Take care! – Alles Gute!

On the telephone – Am Telefon

Hello! – Hallo!
Can I speak with...(please)? – Kann ich mit ... sprechen, (bitte)?
Hang on... – Moment!
...speaking! – Hier ist...
It's me! – Ich bin dran; Ich bin's!
It's ... – Hier ist...
I'm phoning you as we arranged. – Ich wollte Dich doch anrufen.
Can we meet ...? – Kann ich Dich ... treffen?
　this evening – heute abend
　at... o'clock – um... *(see page 21)*
Where? – Wo?
At... – Bei...; Am...; In...
Can you spell it? – Wie schreibt sich das?
OK, thank you! – OK, danke!
See you later! – Bis nachher!; Bis dann!
He is not here! – Er ist nicht da.
Can you phone again... – Kannst Du ... noch mal anrufen?
　later – später
　this afternoon – heute nachmittag

I don't understand. – Ich kann Sie *(formal)*/Dich *(informal)* nicht verstehen.
Do you speak…? – Sprechen Sie…?*(formal)*; Sprichst Du…? *(informal)*
Please speak slowly. – Können Sie *(formal)*/Kannst Du *(informal)* bitte etwas langsamer sprechen?

Health – Gesundheit

I need to see a doctor. – Ich brauche einen Arzt.
doctor – Arzt*(m)*
surgery [UK]; doctor's office [US] – Praxis*(f)*; Arztpraxis*(f)*
chemist [UK]; pharmacy – Apotheke*(f)*
I have… – Ich habe…
I have caught… – Ich habe mich mit…angesteckt.
I think I have… – Ich glaube ich habe…
Do you have something for…? – Haben Sie etwas gegen…?
    gonorrhoea – Gonorrhoe *(f)*; Tripper *(m)*
    syphilis – Syphilis *(f)*
    crabs – Filzläuse *(pl)*
    lice – Läuse *(pl)*
    herpes – Herpes *(m)*
    scabies – Krätze *(f)*
I hurt here. – Es tut hier weh.
I'm bleeding. – Ich blute.
I'm itching. – Es juckt.
My throat/penis/anus hurts. – Mein Hals/Penis/Hintern tut weh.

Services – Dienste

Can you help me? – Können Sie mir helfen? *(formal)*; Kannst Du mir helfen?*(informal)*
How much is this/that? – Was kostet das?
Have you got a map of…? – Haben Sie einen Stadtplan von…?
Have you got a map of the city? – Haben Sie einen Stadtplan?
Can I have the number for Gay Switchboard? – Haben Sie die Nummer vom Gay Switchboard/Schwulenzentrum/Rosa Telefon?
Can I have the number of the AIDS helpline? – Haben Sie die Nummer von der (deutschen)AIDS Hilfe ?*(in Germany)*; Haben Sie die Nummer von der AIDS Hilfe ? *(elsewhere)*
Can you give me the name of a doctor who is experienced in AIDS/HIV-related problems? – Können Sie mir den Namen von einem Arzt geben, der mit AIDS/HIV-verwandten Problemen Erfahrung hat?

Can you give me the name of a clinic which is experienced in AIDS/HIV-related problems? – Können Sie mir den Namen von einer Klinik geben, die mit AIDS/HIV-verwandten Problemen Erfahrung hat?

Can you give me the name of a gay-friendly doctor? – Können Sie mir den Namen eines schwulenfreundlichen Artzes geben?

Excuse me! – Entschuldigung!

Where is/are...? – Wo ist.../sind...?
- **the sauna** – die Sauna
- **the cruising areas** – die Cruising-Zonen
- **the gay bars** – die Schwulenbars; die Schwulenkneipen
- **the cottages [UK]; tea rooms [US]** – die Klappen
- **the gay bookshop** – die schwule Buchhandlung
- **the gay hotels** – die schwulen Hotels

Contact ads – Kleinanzeigen; Inserate

I am... – Ich bin...

I am looking for a ... guy. – Ich suche einen ... Boy /Typ.
(add final -en to adjectives for use in this sentence construction – eg. I am looking for an active guy = Ich suche einen aktiven Boy)

- **active** – aktiv
- **affectionate** – liebevoll; zärtlich
- **athletic** – gut gebaut; athletisch
- **attractive** – attraktiv
- **bisexual** – bisexuell; bi
- **boyish** – jungenhaft; knabenhaft
- **caring** – einfühlsam; warmherzig
- **Christian** – christlich
- **chubby** – mollig
- **clean** – sauber; gepflegt
- **clean-shaven** – glattrasiert
- **conservative** – konservativ
- **considerate** – rücksichtsvoll
- **cuddly** – knuddelig
- **cute** – hübsch
- **discreet** – diskret
- **dominant** – dominant
- **easy-going** – lässig; unkompliziert; salopp
- **educated** – gebildet; kultiviert
- **experienced** – erfahren; ein Experte *(noun)*
- **friendly** – freundlich; sympatisch
- **gentle** – sanft; zärtlich; liebenswürdig
- **good-looking** – gutaussehend
- **hairy** – behaart
- **handsome** – gutaussehend
- **honest** – ehrlich
- **horny** – scharf; geil
- **I have a good sense of humour** – Ich habe einen Sinn für Humor; Ich bin humorvoll; Ich habe viel Humor
- **independent** – selbstständig; unabhängig
- **inexperienced** – unerfahren

intelligent – intelligent
interesting – interessant
introverted – introvertiert; ruhig
lonely – einsam
loyal – treu
married – verheiratet
masculine – maskulin; männlich
mature – reif
of medium build – normal gebaut
middle aged – mittleren Alters; in den mittleren Jahren
military – militärisch
muscular – muskulös; kräftig
a nature lover – ein Naturfreund; naturverbunden
non-scene – kein Szenengänger; kein Szenentyp
a non-smoker – ein Nichtraucher
older – älter
open – offen
open minded – aufgeschlossen; salopp
outgoing – extrovertiert; lebhaft
passionate – leidenschaftlich
passive – passiv
quiet – ruhig
radical – radikal
refined – kultiviert
reliable – zuverlässig
reserved – reserviert; zurückhaltend
romantic – romantisch
of the same age – gleichaltrig
sensitive – einfühlsam; sensibel
serious – seriös; ernsthaft
shy – schüchtern
sincere – aufrichtig
slim – schlank
a smoker – ein Raucher
smooth – unbehaart
special – speziell
spontaneous – spontan; unternehmungslustig
sporty – sportlich
straight acting – natürlich; unauffällig; nicht tuntenhaft; nicht tuntig
straight forward – aufrichtig
a student – (ein) Student
submissive – gelehrig; passiv
tall – groß
transsexual – transsexuell
a university graduate – Akademiker; Hochschulabsolvent
a virgin – unerfahren
warm – warm; warmherzig
well-endowed; well-hung – gut bestückt; großschwänzig
well-built – gut gebaut
young – jung
younger – jünger
youthful – jugendlich

I am looking for a guy... – Ich suche einen Boy/Typ...
with a good sense of humour – mit einen Sinn für Humor; mit viel Humor

I am looking for a ... guy. – Ich suche einen Boy/Typ…
  middle aged – mittleren Alters; in den mittleren Jahren

I am looking for ... – Ich suche …
  a nature lover – einen Naturfreund
  a non-scene guy – keinen Szenengänger; keinen Szenentyp
  a non-smoker – einen Nichtraucher
  a smoker – einen Raucher
  a student – einen Student
  a university graduate – einen Akademiker; einen Hochschulabsolvent

no effeminates – keine Tunten; keine Effeminierte

no fats – keine Dicken

...welcome – gerne…

for friendship – für eine Freundschaft; um eine Freundschaft aufzubauen

for a relationship – für eine Beziehung/Partnerschaft; um eine Beziehung/Partnerschaft aufzubauen

for sex – für Sex; für Fickspiele

...only – nur…

I have... – Ich habe…
  blue eyes – blaue Augen
  brown eyes – braune Augen
  green eyes – grüne Augen
  grey eyes – graue Augen
  blonde hair – blonde Haare
  brown hair – braune Haare
  black hair – schwarze Haare
  red hair – rote Haare
  grey hair – graue Haare
  dark hair – dunkle Haare
  short hair – kurze Haare
  long hair – lange Haare

I have a beard. – Ich habe einen Vollbart; Ich habe einen Bart.

I have a moustache. – Ich habe einen Schnauzer; Ich habe einen Schnurrbart

I'm bald. – Ich habe eine Glatze.

Expressions – Weitere Ausdrücke

My God! – Um Gottes Willen!; Mein Gott!

Fantastic! – Fantastisch!; Spitze!; Toll!; Great!

I'm sorry. – Tut mir leid.

Excuse me! – Entschuldigung!

Get fucked! – Leck mich am Arsch!

Fuck off! – Verpiß Dich!; Hau ab!

Shit! – Scheiße!

Darling! – Schätzchen!; Schatz!; Darling!
My dear! – Herzchen!; mein Lieber!
Honey! – Schätzchen!; Herzchen!
Oh dear! – O jeh!
How wonderful! – Wunderbar!
How awful! – Wie furchtbar!; Wie eklig!; Wie schrecklich!
He's a friend of Dorothy. – Er gehört zur Familie; Er ist ein warmer Bruder.
As camp as knickers. – Sehr tuntenhaft.
Wow! – Wau!

Other useful vocabulary – Zusätzliches nützliches Vokabular

Yes. – Ja.
No. – Nein.
I am... – ich bin...
he is... – er ist...
you are... – Du bist... *(informal)*; Sie sind... *(formal)*
my friend is... – ein Freund von mir ist...
my friends are... – meine Freunde sind...
my boyfriend is... – mein Freund ist...
adult – erwachsene *(adj)*; der Erwachsene *(m. noun)*
AIDS – AIDS
bent [UK]; homo [US] – andersrum
bisexual – bisexuell; bi *(adj)*
a bitch – eine Schlampe*(f)*; eine Zicke*(f)*; ein Miststück *(n)*
to bitch – meckern; lästern
bitchy – gehässig; gemein
body-building – das Body-Building*(noun)*
butch – machohaft; betont männlich *(for women)*; betont maskulin *(for men)*
camp – tuntenhaft; tuntig
to chat someone up – jemanden anmachen
to be 'in the closet' – eine Klemmschwester sein; sein Schwulsein verbergen
come; spunk – das Sperma*(n)*; der Samen*(m)*
to come – kommen; abspritzen
to 'come out' – sein "Coming-Out" haben; outcomen
a cow – eine Kuh*(f)*

to cruise – cruisen
in drag – in Fummel; als Tunte; als Transe
drag shows – Transvestitenshows*(pl)*
a dyke [UK]; a lesbo [US] – eine Lesbe*(f)*
a butch dyke – eine maskuline Lesbe*(f)*; eine Jeanslesbe*(f)*; eine Lederlesbe*(f)*; ein kesser Vater*(m)*; ein Kraftfahrer*(m)*; ein Fernfahrer*(m)*
erect – steif
an erection; hard-on – eine Erektion*(f)*; ein Steifer *(m)*
a fag hag – eine Schwulen-Mutti *(f)*
female – weiblich; Frauen
french-kissing – der Zungenkuß*(f)*
a fuck – ein Fick*(m)*
gay – schwul *(adj)*; der Schwule *(m)*
the gay scene – die Schwulenszene*(f)*
a girl – eine Frau*(f)*
a guy – ein Typ *(m)*; ein Kerl *(m)*; ein Boy *(m)*
the leather scene – die Lederszene*(f)*
a lesbian – eine Lesbe*(f)*; lesbisch *(adj)*
male – männlich *(adj)*; Männer *(noun)*
men only – nur Männer
the nightclub – der Nachtclub*(m)*
the nudist beach – der FKK-Strand (Freikörperkultur)*(m)*
to pick someone up – jemanden aufreißen
to be pissed off with someone – von jemandem die Schnauze voll haben
a poof; a faggot [US] – eine Trine*(f)*
a queen – eine Schwuchtel*(f)*; eine Trine*(f)*; eine Tunte*(f)*
queer – schwul*(adj)*; andersrum*(adj)*
queer-bashing – Schwule klatschen/zusammenschlagen
a rent-boy – ein Rent-Boy *(m)*; ein Stricher *(m)*
SM (sadomasochism) – Sadomasochismus*(m)*; S und M
skinheads – die Skinheads*(pl)*
a slut – ein Flittchen *(n)*
straight – hetero *(adj)*; der Hetero*(m)*; der Heti*(m)*; der Stino*(m)*
a tart – eine Schlampe*(f)*
transvestite – ein Transvestit *(m)*; eine Transe*(f)*; ein Transie *(m)*
a wank; a jerk-off [US] – das Wichsen*(n)*

women only – nur Frauen
one – eins
two – zwei
three – drei
four – vier
five – fünf
six – sechs
seven – sieben
eight – acht
nine – neun
ten – zehn
eleven – elf
twelve – zwölf
thirteen dreizehn
fourteen – vierzehn
fifteen – fünfzehn
sixteen – sechzehn
seventeen – siebzehn
eighteen – achtzehn
nineteen – neunzehn
twenty – zwanzig
twenty one – einundzwanzig
twenty two – zweiundzwanzig
thirty – dreißig
forty – vierzig
fifty – fünzig
sixty – sechzig
seventy – siebzig
eighty – achtzig
ninety – neunzig
one hundred – hundert
one thousand – tausend

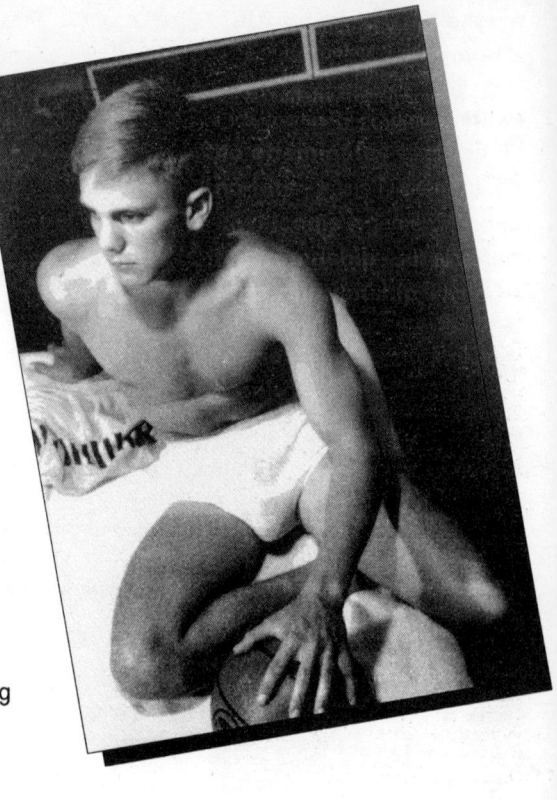

Talking safer sex!

On the telephone – Am Telefon

Hello, Switchboard. John speaking. Can I help you?
Hallo, John vom Switchboard. Kann ich Dir helfen?

Um...hello. Um, can I ask you some questions?
Äh...hallo. Äh, kann ich Dir einige Fragen stellen?

Yes, go on.
Ja, gern.

Well, it's a bit embarassing.
Nun, es ist mir ein wenig peinlich.

Don't worry about it
Mach Dir keine Gedanken.

It's about AIDS and that...
Es geht um AIDS und so...

OK.
Ja, OK.

I know everyone says you should wear a condom to well...you know...fuck.
Ich weiß, daß alle sagen, daß man beim, - na ja, ficken ein Kondom benutzen sollte.

Yes, that's right. They are good protection against HIV and other little nasties.
Ja, das stimmt, Kondome sind ein guter Schutz gegen HIV und andere kleine "Ungeheuer".

Yes, but does that make it totally safe?
Ja, aber machen denn Kondome Sex total safe?

No, nothing is going to make it one hundred percent safe. But they do cut down the risk.
Nein, es gibt nichts was ihn hundert Prozent sicher machen kann. Aber Kondome halten das Risiko niedrig.

So I could still be infected, even if I use a condom?
So könnte ich also trotz Kondom infiziert werden?

Well yes, the condom could break, could be faulty or could come off. But if you use them properly, the chances are pretty slim. So when you fuck, make sure you always use a condom.
Nun ja, das Kondom könnte reißen, könnte fehlerhaft sein oder runterrutschen, aber wenn Du es richtig benutzt ist die Wahrscheinlichkeit ziemlich gering, daß was passiert. Pass also auf, daß Du beim Ficken immer ein Kondom benutzt.

What about oral sex?
Wie ist es mit oralem Sex?

Well that's a harder one. Most people believe that there's what they call a theoretical risk to sucking without condoms.
Nun, das ist schon etwas schwieriger. Die meisten Leute glauben, daß es ein theoretisches Risiko beim Oralsex gibt.

What does that mean?
Und was heißt das?

Good question. I think it means that nobody is going to say you will never transmit HIV that way but the chances are so small, they are not worth worrying about. You can take extra care by keeping your mouth clean and healthy and maybe by not taking cum in your mouth but that is up to you. I can tell you though that I never use a condom when sucking.
Gute Frage. Ich denke das bedeutet, daß wohl niemand sagen wird, daß man auf diesem Wege niemals HIV übertragen kann, jedoch ist die Wahrscheinlichkeit so gering, daß man sich darüber keinen Kopf zerbrechen braucht. Man kann besonders vorsichtig sein, indem man seinen Mund sauber und gesund hält und vielleicht auch kein Sperma in den Mund nimmt, aber das ist ganz Dir überlassen. Ich kann Dir aber sagen, daß ich beim Blasen nie ein Kondom benutze.

Oh.
Oh.

Well, has that been helpful?
Nun, war das hilfreich?

Yes it has. I just get confused, there is so much information about.
Ja, das war es. Ich bin nur ein wenig durcheinander - so viele Infos auf einmal...

Yes, I know. Talk to your friends about it. We're all in the same boat and you can always call us again if you think of anything else.
Ja, ich weiß. Sprich mit Deinen Freunden darüber. Wir sitzen alle im selben Boot und Du kannst uns jederzeit wieder anrufen, wenn es noch etwas anderes gibt.

Great, thanks a lot. Bye!
Vielen Dank! Tschüß!

Bye!
Tschüß!

Spanish
(with Latin American Spanish)

NOTE: [SP] = used in Spain; [L.AM] = used in Latin America; [MEX] = used in Mexico

The Bar/Club – El Bar

I would like... please. – (Me pones)... por favor.
- **a half-pint [UK]** – una caña; una media jarra [MEX]
- **a pint [UK]** – un tubo; una jarra [MEX]
- **a beer** – una cerveza
- **a light beer** – una cerveza suave/ligera
- **a heavy beer [UK]** – una cerveza negra/fuerte
- **a shandy** – una cerveza clara; un shandy
- **a glass of red wine** – una copa/un vaso de vino tinto; un tinto
- **a glass of white wine** – una copa/un vaso de vino blanco; un vino blanco; un blanco
- **a gin and tonic** – un gin-tonic
- **a vodka** – un vodka
- **a vodka and coke /orange** – un vodka con coca-cola/naranja
- **a whisky; a scotch [US]** – un whisky
- **a rum** – un ron
- **a cider** – una sidra
- **a coke** – una coca (cola)
- **a lemonade** – una gaseosa
- **an orange juice** – un zumo de naranja [SP]; un jugo de naranja [L.AM]
- **an apple juice** – un zumo de manzana [SP]; un jugo de manzana [L.AM]
- **a mineral water** – un agua mineral
- **a coffee** – un café
- **white coffee** – café con leche
- **a tea** – un té
- **hot/cold milk** – un vaso de leche caliente/fría
- **a hot chocolate** – un chocolate caliente

with/without – con.../sin...
- **sugar** – azúcar
- **milk** – leche
- **ice** – hielo
- **water** – agua
- **soda** – soda
- **tonic** – tonica
- **blackcurrant** – zumo de grosella negra [SP]; jugo de grosella negra [L.AM]
- **lemon juice** – zumo de limón [SP]; jugo de limón [L.AM]

How much is that? – ¿Cuánto es?

Is this seat free? – ¿Está libre este asiento?
- **Yes (it's free).** – Sí (está libre).
- **No (it's taken).** – No (está ocupado).

Where are the toilets? – ¿Dondé están los servicios? [SP]; ¿Dondé está el baño? [L.AM]
- **at the back** – al fondo

on the right – a la derecha
on the left – a la izquierda
downstairs – abajo
upstairs – arriba

Do you sell anything to eat? – ¿Tiene algo para comer?

something hot/cold – algo caliente/frío

Have you got a menu? – ¿Me trae la carta?; ¿Me trae el menú?

Do you sell...? – ¿Venden…?
  matches – fósforos; cerillas [SP]
  cigarettes – cigarillos; cigarros
  poppers – poppers
  condoms; rubbers [US] – preservativos; condones; gomas [SP]; forros [L.AM]
  lubricant – lubricante

What time does this place close/open? – ¿A qué hora cierra/abre este bar?

At...o'clock – A las… en punto; A la… en punto *(with one o'clock)*
  one – una
  two – dos
  three – tres
  four – cuatro
  five – cinco
  six – seis
  seven – siete
  eight – ocho
  nine – nueve
  ten – diez
  eleven – once
  twelve – doce; mediodía *(midday)*;
      medianoche *(midnight)*
  half past one – una y media

Cruising – Ligue

Hi! – ¡Hola!; ¿Qué tal?

Hello! – ¡Hola!

Good evening. – Buenas noches.

How are you? – ¿Cómo estás?
  good – bien
  OK – OK

Do you speak… – ¿Hablas…?
  English – inglés
  French – francés
  German – alemán
  Italian – italiano
  Spanish – español
  Dutch – holandés
  Portuguese – portugués

Yes (I speak...). – Sí (hablo…).
  a bit – un poco; algo

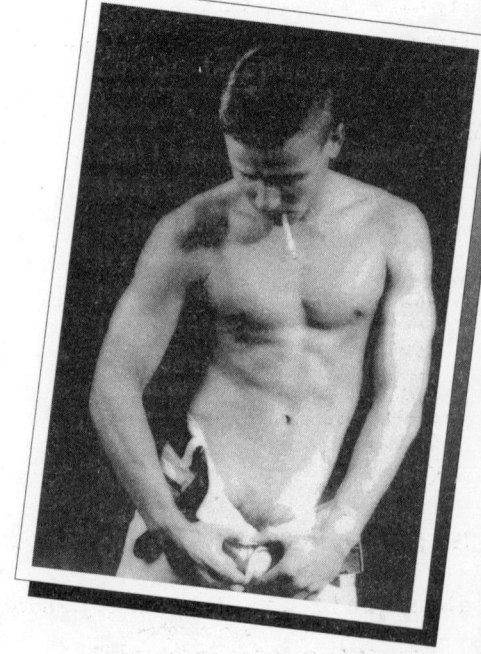

No (I don't speak...). – No (no hablo...).

I'm sorry, I don't speak... – Lo siento, no hablo...

I don't understand. – No entiendo (nada).

Can you repeat that (please)? – ¿Te importa repetirlo, por favor? *(informal)*; ¿Le importa repetirlo, por favor? *(formal)*

Can you speak more slowly please? – ¿Te importa hablar más despacio, por favor? *(informal)*; ¿Le importa hablar más despacio, por favor? *(formal)*

Have you got a light? – ¿Tienes fuego?

Have you got the time? – ¿Tienes hora?; ¿Qué hora es, por favor?

Thank you! – ¡Gracias!

Are you on your own? – ¿Estás solo?; ¿Andas solo?; ¿Has venido solo?; ¿Vienes solo?

I'm with my boyfriend. – Estoy con mi pareja/amigo/novio.

I'm with a friend/friends. – Estoy con un amigo. *(male friend)*; Estoy con una amiga. *(female friend)*/Estoy con amigos. *(male friends)*; Estoy con amigas. *(female friends)*

What's your name? – ¿Cómo te llamas?

My name is... – Me llamo...

Where do you come from? – ¿De dónde eres?

I come from... – Soy de...
    England – Inglaterra
    Scotland – Escocia
    Wales – Gales
    Britain – Gran Bretaña
    Ireland – Irlanda
    France – Francia
    Germany – Alemania
    Spain – España
    Portugal – Portugal
    Italy – Italia
    Switzerland – Suiza
    Belgium – Bélgica
    Austria – Austria
    Holland – Holanda
    the United States – Estados Unidos
    Canada – Canadá
    Japan – Japón
    Australia – Australia
    New Zealand – Nueva Zelanda

Do you come here often? – ¿Vienes (aquí) a menudo?; ¿Has estado aquí muchas veces?

Would you like...? – ¿Quieres... ?; ¿Te apetece...?; Te gustaría...?
    a drink – tomar algo; algo de beber
    a cigarette – un cigarillo; un cigarro [SP]

(No, thank you) I don't smoke. – (No gracias,) no fumo.

Are you on holiday [UK]/vacation [US]? – ¿Estás de vacaciones?
    Yes (I'm on holiday [UK]/vacation [US]). – Sí (estoy de vacaciones).
    (No) I work here. – (No) trabajo aquí.
    I study here. – Estudio aquí.

Where do you live? – ¿Dónde vives?

Where are you staying? – ¿Dónde te alojas?; ¿En dónde estás?

I live... – Vivo...

I'm staying... – Estoy...
    with friends – en casa de amigos *(male friends)*/amigas *(female friends)*
    in a hotel – en un hotel
    in a flat [UK]/apartment [US] – en un piso [SP]; en un departamento [L.AM]
    in a house – en una casa

Would you like to go...? – ¿Quieres ir...?
    to a cafe – a un café
    to a restaurant – a un restaurante
    to another bar – a otro bar
    to a disco – a una disco/discoteca
    to a sauna – a una sauna
    to the beach – a la playa
    to the pool – a la piscina; a la alberca [MEX]
    for a walk – de paseo [SP]; a caminar [L.AM]

Would you like to... with me? – ¿Quieres... conmigo?
    dance – bailar
    have a drink – tomar algo de beber [SP]; tomar algo [L.AM]
    have something to eat – comer algo

Can I buy you a drink? – ¿Te puedo invitar a algo de beber?; ¿Quieres tomar algo? [L.AM]

What would you like (to drink)? – ¿Qué tomas (de beber)?; ¿Tomas algo (de beber)?

It's... here tonight, (isn't it)? – ¿Está... esta noche (no)?
    packed – a tope; hasta los topes; muy lleno
    busy – animado; concurrido; guay; lleno
    dead – muerto; vacío
    boring – aburrido

I like your... – Me gusta tu...
    jacket – chaqueta
    shirt – camisa
    clothes – ropa
    haircut – corte de pelo

Where did you get it/them from? – ¿Dónde la compraste?

Where did you get your hair done? – ¿Dónde te cortaste el pelo?

You look very nice tonight! – ¡Estás muy guapo [SP]/lindo [L.AM] esta noche!

How old are you? – ¿Cuántos años tienes?

I'm... (years old). – Tengo... años. *(see numbers on p55)*

Nice eyes! – ¡Vaya ojos!; ¡Qué ojos!; ¡Bonitos ojos!; ¡Qué lindos ojos! [L.AM]
Nice legs! – ¡Vaya piernas!; ¡Qué piernas!; ¡Bonitas piernas! ¡Qué lindas piernas! [L.AM]
Nice bum! – ¡ Vaya culo/trasero/cola [L.AM]!; ¡Qué culo/trasero/cola [L.AM]!; ¡Buen culo/trasero/cola [L.AM]!; ¡Qué lindo culo! [L.AM]
What a nice smile you have! – ¡Qué sonrisa tan bonita tienes!
    You're beautiful. – ¡Qué guapo eres! [SP]; ¡Qué lindo eres! [L.AM]
    You're handsome. – ¡Eres guapo! [SP]; ¡Qué guapo eres! [SP]; ¡Qué lindo eres! [L.AM]
    You're hunky. – ¡Qué fuerte estás!; ¡Qué guapo estás!; ¡Qué cachas estás![SP]
    You're a hunk. – ¡Qué macho (estás)!; ¡Qué machote (estás)!; ¡Qué tiarrón (estás)! [SP]; ¡Qué pedazo de tío! [SP] ¡Qué buenote (estás)! [L.AM]; ¡Qué buenísimo (estás)! [L.AM]; ¡Qué bueno que estás! [L.AM]
    You're gorgeous. – ¡Estás muy bueno!; ¡Estás como un camión/un tren/un queso/un pan! [SP]
    You're sweet. – ¡Qué tierno eres!; ¡Qué dulce eres!
    You're cute. – ¡Qué lindo eres!
    You're sexy. – ¡Qué sexy eres!
    You're attractive. – ¡Qué atractivo eres!
You really turn me on. – ¡ Como me estás poniendo!; ¡Me pones a cien!; ¡Me pones cachondo! [SP]
You really make me hot. – ¡Me pones caliente!; ¡Me calientas! [L.AM]
I'm crazy about you. – ¡Estoy loco por ti!
You're not my type. – No eres mi tipo.
I'm not interested. – – No me interesas.
Get lost! – ¡Piérdete!; ¡ Vete por ahí !; ¡Vete!; ¡Lárgate!
Piss off! – ¡ Déjame en paz!; ¡ Pesado!; ¡ Vete a tomar por el culo ! [SP]; ¡Dejate de joder! [SP]; ¡Vete a la chingada! [MEX]
What type of guys do you like? – ¿Qué tipo de chico te gusta?
What are you into? – ¿Qué te gusta?
I'm into...; I like...*(plural nouns)* – Me gustan...
I'm not into...; I don't like...*(plural nouns)* – No me gustan...
    older men – hombres mayores; hombres maduros
    younger men – jovencitos; chicos jóvenes
    blonde guys – los rubios
    guys with brown hair – los castaños
    guys with dark hair – los morenos; los morochos [L.AM]
    red heads – los pelirrojos
    guys with short hair – los hombres con el pelo corto
    guys with long hair – los hombres con el pelo largo
    hunky guys; well-built guys – los hombres fuertes; los muchachotes [SP]
    thin guys – los hombres delgados
    chubby guys – los hombres gorditos
    tall guys – los hombres altos
    short guys – los hombres bajos
    guys with dark eyes – los hombres con ojos oscuros
    guys with blue eyes – los hombres con ojos azules
    denim – los vaqueros; me va el rollo tejano *(I'm into denim)*

    dildos – los consoladores
    tatoos – los tatuajes
    boots – los botas (militares)
    uniforms – los uniformes
    threesomes – los tríos; los menage à trois; las camas de tres [L.AM]

I'm into…; I like…*(singular nouns)* – Me gusta…

I'm not into…; I don't like…*(singular nouns)* – No me gusta…
    leather – el cuero; la ropa de cuero
    rubber – la (ropa de) goma
    water sports – la lluvia dorada; la ducha dorada
    fisting – el fist-fucking; el fisting
    cross-dressing – transvestirme; el transvestismo
    piercing – ponerme anillos en el cuerpo
    brown; scat – que me caguen encima; la escatofilia
    bondage – ser esclavo; ser tu esclavo *(me to you)*; que fueras mi esclavo *(you to me)*

Is there somewhere quieter/more private we can go? – ¿Hay algún sitio donde podamos estar más tranquilos/más privados?

Do you want to come to my place? – ¿Quieres venir a (mi) casa?; ¿Quieres venir conmigo?

Yes. – Sí.

I'm sorry, I can't. – Lo siento, no puedo.

Can we meet again? – ¿Podemos vernos otra vez?

When? – ¿Cuándo?

Would you like to meet me…? – ¿Quieres que quedemos/nos encontremos/nos veamos…?
    this evening – esta noche
    tomorrow – mañana
    tomorrow morning – mañana por la mañana
    tomorrow afternoon – mañana por la tarde
    tomorrow night – mañana por la noche
    on Monday – el lunes
    on Tuesday – el martes
    on Wednesday – el miércoles
    on Thursday – el jueves
    on Friday – el viernes
    on Saturday – el sábado
    on Sunday – el domingo

At what time? – ¿A qué hora? *(see page 40)*

at… o'clock – a las… en punto; a la… en punto *(used with one o'clock)*

where? – ¿dónde?
    here – aquí
    at my hotel – en mi hotel
    at my flat [UK]/apartment [US] – en mi piso [SP]; en mi departamento [L.AM]
    at my house – en mi casa
    at my friend's place – en casa de un amigo
    at your place – en tu casa

Can I have your phone number? – ¿Puedes darme tu número de teléfono?; ¡Dame tu número de teléfono!

Can I have your address? – ¿Puedes darme tu dirección?; ¡Dame tu dirección!
Bye. – ¡Adiós!; ¡Chao!
Goodbye. – ¡Adiós!
See you again! – ¡Hasta luego!; ¡Hasta la vista!; ¡Hasta pronto!;

At his place/your place – En su casa/tu casa

Would you like some..? – ¿Quieres tomar...?
   coffee – un café
   tea – un té
   wine – un vino
   orange juice – un zumo de naranja [SP]; un jugo de naranja [L.AM]

Would you like something to eat? – ¿Quieres comer algo?; ¿Quieres algo de comer?

Are you hungry/thirsty? – ¿Tienes hambre/sed?

Are you cold/too hot? – ¿Tienes frío/demasiado calor?

Do you want to watch TV/a video? – ¿Quieres ver la tele/un video?

Would you like to listen to some music? – ¿Quieres que ponga música?; Quieres escuchar música?

What kind of music do you like? – ¿Qué tipo de música te gusta?
   classical – la música clásica
   opera – la ópera
   jazz – el jazz
   rock – el rock
   pop – el pop
   folk – el folclore
   traditional – la música tradicional

Can I kiss you? – ¿Te puedo dar un beso?

Would you like...? – ¿Te hago...?; ¿Quieres...?
   a massage – un masage
   a blow job – una mamada; una chupada

What do you like doing? – ¿Qué te gustaría hacer?

I like... – Me gusta...

I don't like... – No me gusta...
   kissing – besar
   cuddling – abrazar
   fucking – joder; follar [SP]; coger [L.AM]; chingar [MEX]
   being fucked – que me jodan; que me follen [SP]; que me cojan [L.AM]; que me chingen [MEX]
   sucking – chupar; mamar
   being sucked – que me la chupen; que me la mamen
   wanking; jerking off [US] – masturbarme *(alone)*/masturbarte *(me to you)*; hacerme una paja *(alone)*/hacerte una paja *(me to you)*
   mutual masturbation – la masturbación mútua
   licking – lamer
   stroking – acariciar

rubbing – frotar
spanking – dar palmadas (en el culo); zurrar [SP]; dar cachetes [SP]
being spanked – que me des palmadas (en el culo); que me zurres [SP]; que me des cachetes [SP]
cross-dressing – transvestirme; vestirme de mujer
shaving – afeitarme *(shaving myself)*; afeitarte *(me to you)*
fisting – el fist-fucking; el fisting
rimming – chupar el culo; besos negros; lamer el culo

Do you like..? – ¿Quieres…?; ¿Te gustaría…?; ¿Te apetecería…?
kissing – que nos besemos *(reciprocal)*; que te bese *(me to you)*; besarme *(you to me)*
cuddling – que nos abracemos *(reciprocal)*; que te abrace *(me to you)*; abrazarme *(you to me)*
fucking – que jodamos/que follemos [SP]/que cojamos [L.AM]/que chingemos [MEX] *(reciprocal)*; joderme/follarme [SP]/ cogerme [L.AM]/chingarme [MEX] *(you to me)*
being fucked – que te joda/que te folle [SP]/que te coja [L.AM]/que te chinge [MEX] *(me to you)*
sucking – que nos la chupemos/que nos la mamemos *(reciprocal)*; chupármela/mamármela *(you to me)*
being sucked – que te la chupe/que te la mame *(me to you)*
wanking – que te haga una paja *(me to you)*; hacerme una paja *(you to me)*
mutual masturbation – que nos la meneemos; que nos masturbemos
licking – que nos lamamos [SP]/lamemos [L.AM] *(reciprocal)*; que te lama [SP]/lame [L.AM] *(me to you)*
stroking – que nos acariciemos *(reciprocal)*; que te acaricie *(me to you)*; acariciarme *(you to me)*
rubbing – que nos frotemos *(reciprocal)*; que te frote *(me to you)*; frotarme *(you to me)*
spanking – que nos demos palmadas (en el culo)/que nos zurremos el culo [SP] *(reciprocal)*; darme palmadas en el culo/zurrarme el culo [SP] *(you to me)*
being spanked – que te de palmadas (en el culo)/que te zurre [SP] *(me to you)*
cross-dressing – vestirte de mujer; ¿Te gusta transvestirte?
shaving – que nos afeitemos *(reciprocal)*; que te afeite *(me to you)*; afeitarme *(you to me)*
fisting – meterme el puño por el culo *(you to me)*; que te meta el puño por el culo *(me to you)*
rimming – que te lama [SP]/lame [L.AM] el culo *(me to you)*; que te chupe el culo *(me to you)*; lamerme el culo *(you to me)*; chuparme el culo *(you to me)*

Are you experienced? – ¿Tienes mucha experiencia?

I am experienced. – Tengo mucha experiencia.

Are you inexperienced? – ¿No tienes mucha experiencia?; ¿Eres inexperto?

I am inexperienced. – No tengo mucha experiencia; Soy inexperto.

I like to be… – Prefierio ser…
active – activo
passive – pasivo

Shall we go to the bedroom/bathroom? – ¿Vamos a la cama/al baño?

Have you got any…? – ¿Tienes…?
condoms; rubbers [US] – preservativos; condones; gomas [SP]; forros [L.AM]
toys – juguetes (sexuales); fetiches
lubricant – lubricante
poppers – poppers

Are you into safer sex? – ¿Practicas el sexo seguro?

I'm only into safer sex. – Sólo practico el sexo seguro.

I'm HIV-positive. – Soy seropositivo.

Are you HIV-positive? – ¿Eres seropositivo?
Would you like a shower (with me)? – ¿Quieres ducharte (conmigo)?
Take off your...! – ¡Sácate...!; ¡Quítate...!
Can I take off your...? – ¿Puedo sacarte...?; ¿Puedo quitarte...?
   clothes – la ropa
   shirt – la camisa
   trousers; pants [US] – los pantalones
   socks – los calcetines [SP]; las medias [L.AM]
   briefs; underpants; shorts [US] – el slip; los calzoncillos
Lie down! – ¡Échate!; ¡Acuéstate!
Bend over! – ¡Agáchate!; ¡Dóblate hacia delante!
Sit down! – ¡Siéntate!
You're really nice. – Eres muy guapo [SP]/lindo [L.AM].
I like... (singular nouns) – Me gusta...
   your cock – tu pija; tu pito; tu carajo; tu polla [SP]; tu picha [SP]; tu verga [L.AM]
   your bum – tu culo
   your body – tu cuerpo
   your figure – tu talle; tu figura
   your (hairy) chest – tu pecho (peludo)
I like your...(plural nouns) – Me gustan...
   your balls – tus huevos; tus pelotas; tus cojones [SP]; tus bolas [L. AM]
   your nipples – tus pezones; tus tetillas
   your legs – tus piernas
Can I kiss your...? – ¿Puedo besarte...?
Can I suck your...? – ¿Puedo chuparte...?
Can I touch your...? – ¿Puedo tocarte...?
Can I feel your...? – ¿Puedo acariciarte...?
   cock – la pija; el pito; el carajo; la polla [SP]; la picha [SP]; la verga [L.AM]
   balls – los huevos; los pelotas; los cojones [SP]; los bolas [L.AM]
   bum – el culo
   body – el cuerpo
   nipples – los pezones; las tetillas
   (hairy) chest – el pecho (peludo)
   legs – las piernas
   toe – el dedo gordo del pie
That feels good! – ¡Me gusta esto!
That's great! – ¡Genial!; ¡De puta madre!; ¡Qué padre! [MEX]
That's wonderful! – ¡Qué maravilla!; ¡Qué fantástico!
That's really good! – ¡Qué bien!; ¡Muy bueno!; ¡Muy bien!; ¡Qué bueno!
Do that again! – ¡Hazlo otra vez!; ¡Hazlo de nuevo!
My god, that's wonderful! – ¡Lo haces muy bien!;¡Joder, qué pasada! [SP]
Yes...yes... – Más...más...; Sí...sí...
Come on! – Vamos, vamos!¡ Venga, venga!

Fuck me! – ¡Jódeme!; Fóllame! [SP]; ¡Cógeme! [L.AM]; ¡Chíngame! [MEX]
Suck me! – ¡Chúpamela!; ¡Mámamela!
Wank me! – ¡Hazme una paja!; ¡Mastúrbame!
Spank me! – ¡Pégame (en el culo)!; ¡Dame palmadas (en el culo)!; ¡Zúrrame! [SP]
Harder, harder! – ¡Más fuerte!; ¡Más, más!; ¡Más duro!
Slower, slower! – ¡Más despacio!; ¡Mas despacito!
I'm coming…! – ¡Que me corro…! [SP]; ¡Me voy a correr…! [SP]; ¡Me vengo…! [L.AM]; ¡Que me vengo…! [L.AM]
Come all over me! – ¡Córrete encima mío! [SP]; ¡Vente sobre mí! [L.AM]; ¡Vente encima! [L.AM]
I don't like that! – ¡No me gusta eso!
Stop! – ¡Para!; ¡Detente!
That hurts! – ¡Eso duele!; ¡Me duele!
Not so fast/hard! – ¡No tan rápido/fuerte!
Don't come in my mouth/arse! – ¡No te corras en la boca/el culo! [SP]; ¡No te vengas en mi boca/mi culo! [L.AM]
That was wonderful. – Ha estado fantástico; Estuvo fantástico; Fué buenísimo.
Would you like to clean yourself up? – ¿Quieres limpiarte?
Have you got any tissues/a towel? – ¿Tienes papel higíenico/una toalla?
Here you are! – ¡Aquí tienes!
May I use your shower? – ¿Puedo usar la ducha? [SP]; ¿Puedo usar el baño? [L.AM]
Shall we have a shower together? – ¿Nos duchamos juntos?; ¿Nos bañamos juntos? [L.AM]
Can I have a towel (please)? – ¿Me pasas una toalla?
Good night! – ¡Buenas noches! [SP]; ¡Hasta mañana! [L.AM]
Sleep well! – ¡Que duermas bien!
I love you. – Te amo; Te quiero.
Did you sleep well? – ¿Has dormido bien?; ¿Durmío bien?; ¿Dormiste bien? [L.AM]
I'll have to ask you to leave now. – Lo siento, pero tendrías que irte; Lo siento, pero pienso que debes irte.
Can you go now please? – Por favor, vete; ¿Puedes irte ahora, por favor?
I have to go now. – Bueno, me tengo que ir; Tengo que irme.
Would you like some breakfast? – ¿Quieres desayunar?; ¿Quieres algo de desayuno?
Can I write to you? – ¿Puedo escribirte?

It's been nice knowing you! – Me ha encantado conocerte; Me ha gustado conocerte; Me encanta haberte conocido.

Would you like to see me again? – ¿Quieres que nos veamos otra vez?

Can I see you again? – ¿Puedo volver a verte?

Goodbye! – ¡Adiós!; ¡Adiós, nos vemos!

See you again! – ¡Hasta luego!; ¡Espero volver a verte!; ¡Nos vemos luego!

Take care. – Que vaya bien; Cuídate.

On the telephone – Al teléfono

Hello! – ¡Hola!; ¡Diga! [SP]; ¡Dígame! [SP]; ¡Aló! [L.AM]; ¡Bueno! [MEX]

Can I speak with... (please)? – ¿Está... (por favor)?; ¿Puedo hablar con... (por favor)?

Hang on... – Un momentito; Un momento

...speaking! – Hola, soy...

It's me! – ¡Sí, soy yo!

It's... – Hola, soy...

I'm phoning you as we arranged. – Te llamo como acordamos/quedamos.

Can we meet... – Podemos quedar...; podemos vernos...
  this evening – esta noche
  at... o'clock – a las...; *or* a la... *(with one o'clock) (see page 40)*

Where? – ¿Dónde?

At... – En...

Can you spell it? – ¿Cómo se escribe eso?

OK, thank you! – ¡OK, gracias!

See you later! – ¡Hasta luego!; ¡Hasta la vista!; ¡Hasta pronto!; ¡Nos vemos!

He is not here! – ¡No está aquí!

Can you phone again (at)... ? – ¿Puedes llamar...?
  later – más tarde
  this afternoon – esta tarde

I don't understand. – No entiendo.

Do you speak...? – ¿Habla (usted)...?*(formal)*; ¿Hablas...?*(informal)*

Please speak slowly. – Hable despacio por favor. *(formal)*; Habla despacio por favor. *(informal)*

Health – Salud

I need to see a doctor. – Necesito un médico.

doctor – médico; doctor

surgery [UK]; doctor's office [US] – médico consultorio; consulta médica
chemist [UK]; pharmacy – farmacia; droguería [L.AM]
I have... – Tengo...
I have caught... – Me he contagiado de...; He cogido...
I think I have... – Creo que tengo...
Do you have something for...? – ¿Tendría /Tiene algo para...?
    gonorrhoea – la blenorragia; la gonorrea
    syphilis – la sífilis
    crabs – las ladillas
    lice – los piojos
    herpes – el herpes
    scabies – la sarna
I hurt here. – Me duele aquí.
I'm bleeding. – Estoy sangrando.
I'm itching. – Me pica.
My throat/penis/anus hurts. – Me duele la garganta/el pene/el ano.

Services – Ayudas

Can you help me? – ¿Podría ayudarme? *(formal)*; ¿Podrías ayudarme? *(informal)*
How much is this/that? – ¿Cuanto cuesta esto/eso?
Have you got a map of...? – ¿Tiene un mapa/un plano de...?
the city – la ciudad
Can I have the number for Gay Switchboard? – ¿ Me puede dar el número de la centralita gay?; ¿ Me puede dar el número del teléfono gay?
Can I have the number of the AIDS helpline? – ¿ Puede darme el número de la linea de ayuda del SIDA?
Can you give me the name of a doctor who is experienced in AIDS/HIV-related problems? – ¿Puede darme el nombre de un doctor especializado en los problemas relacionados con el SIDA/la seropositividad?
Can you give me the name of a clinic which is experienced in AIDS/HIV-related problems? – ¿Puede darme el nombre de una clinica especializada en los problemas relacionados con el SIDA/la seropositividad?
Can you give me the name of a gay-friendly doctor? – ¿Puedes darme el nombre de algún médico simpatizante con los gays?
Excuse me! – ¡Perdon!
Where is/are...? – ¿Dónde está.../están...?
    the sauna – la sauna
    the cruising areas – las zonas de ligue; las zonas de ambiente; las zonas de encuentro
    the gay bars – los bares gays
    the cottages [UK]; tea rooms [US] – los baños publicos da ambiente; ¿Dónde hay rollo de lavabos? *(Where are the cottages/tea rooms?)*

the gay bookshop – la librería gay
the gay hotels – los hoteles gays

Contact ads – Contactos

I am... – Soy...

I am looking for a...guy – Busco un tipo/hombre...

active – activo
affectionate – cariñoso; afectuoso
athletic – atlético
attractive – atractivo
bisexual – bisexual
boyish – de facciones jóvenes; juvenil; sardino [L.AM]; chamo [L.AM]
caring – afectuoso; bondadoso; considerado
Christian – cristiano
chubby – rellenito; rechoncho; redondo; gordito
clean – limpio; aseado
clean-shaven – sin barba ni bigote; todo afeitado; (*I am... Estoy todo afeitado*).
conservative – conservador
considerate – considerado; atento; comedido
cuddly – mimoso
cute – lindo; bonito; tierno [L.AM]
discreet – discreto
dominant – dominante
easy-going – poco complicado; facil; afable [SP]; descomplicado [L.AM]
educated – culto; educado
experienced – experimentado; con experiencia
friendly – simpático; amable
gentle – gentil; considerado [SP]; tierno [SP]
good-looking – de buen ver; guapo [SP]; lindo [L.AM]; simpático [L.AM]
hairy – peludo
handsome – guapo [SP]; lindo [L.AM]; simpático [L.AM]
honest – honesto; honrado; recto [SP]
horny – caliente; cachondo [SP]; buenote [L.AM]; bueno [L.AM]
with a good sense of humour – con buen sentido del humor; Tengo buen sentido del humor(*I have a good sense of humour*)
independent – independiente
inexperienced – inexperto
intelligent – inteligente
interesting – interesante
introverted – introvertido
lonely – solitario
loyal – leal
married – casado; Estoy casado (*I am married*)
masculine – masculino; varonil
mature – maduro; hecho
of medium build – de tamaño medio
middle aged – de mediana edad; de edad madura
military – militar
muscular – musculoso; fornido; cachas [SP]; fuerte [L.AM]
a nature lover – amante de la naturaleza; amigo de la naturaleza
non-scene – fuera del ambiente; no involucrado en el ambiente
(a) non-smoker – (un) no fumador

older – mayor
open – abierto; sin prejuicios
open minded – libre de prejuicios; imparcial; liberado
outgoing – extrovertido
passionate – apasionado
passive – pasivo
quiet – callado; tranquillo
radical – radical
refined – fino; culto
reliable – de confianza; de fiar; fiable
reserved – reservado
romantic – romántico
of the same age – de la misma edad
sensitive – sensible; tierno; delicado [SP]
serious – serio
shy – timido
sincere – sincero
slim – delgado; esbelto
(a) smoker – (un) fumador
smooth – suave; fino; delicado
special – especial
spontaneous – espontáneo
sporty – deportista
straight acting – no afeminado; viril; macho
straight forward – sencillo; franco; directo; abierto
(a) student – (un) estudiante; (un) universitario
submissive – sumiso
tall – alto
transsexual – transexual
(a) university graduate – licenciado; con carrera
(a) virgin – (un) virgen
warm – afectuoso; amigable
well-endowed; well-hung – bien dotado
well-built – fornido; bien hecho
young – jóven
younger – más jóven
youthful – juvenil

no effeminates – no afeminados; abstenerse afeminados

no fats – no gordos; abstenerse gordos

...welcome – ...bienvenido(s) (-s *if plural*)

for friendship – para amistad

for a relationship – para (una) relación

for sex – para sexo

...only – sólo...; solamente...

I have... – Tengo...
    blue eyes – los ojos azules
    brown eyes – los ojos marrones/castaños
    green eyes – los ojos verdes
    grey eyes – los ojos grises
    blonde hair – el pelo rubio

brown hair – el pelo castaño
black hair – el pelo negro
red hair – Soy pelirojo. *(I have red hair.)*
grey hair – el pelo gris
dark hair – el pelo moreno
short hair – el pelo corto
long hair – el pelo largo

I have a beard. – Tengo barba.

I have a moustache. – Tengo bigote.

I'm bald. – Soy calvo.

Expressions – Espresiones

My God! – ¡Dios mío!

Fantastic! – ¡Fantástico!

I'm sorry. – Lo siento.

Excuse me! – ¡Perdón!

Get fucked! – ¡Que te folle un pez! [SP]; ¡Que te jodan! [SP]; ¡Que te cojan! [L.AM]

Fuck off! – ¡Vete a la mierda!; ¡Vete al carajo! [L.AM]; ¡Que te den por el culo!

Shit! – ¡Mierda!; ¡Carajo! [L.AM]

Darling! – ¡Querido!; ¡Cariño!; ¡Pedazo del corazón!; ¡Mi amor!

My dear! – ¡Encanto!

Honey! – ¡Guapo!; ¡Lindo!; ¡Mi cielo!; ¡Cariñito!

Oh dear! – ¡Dios mio!; ¡Vaya por dios! [SP]

How wonderful! – ¡Qué bien!; ¡Qué maravilloso!; ¡Qué precioso!; ¡Qué bueno!

How awful! – ¡Qué horrible!; ¡Qué desastre!; ¡Qué terrible!

He's a friend of Dorothy. – Ese/el entiende; Otro que tal baila.

As camp as knickers. – ¡Tiene una pluma que te cagas!

Wow! – ¡Ay,ay,ay!; ¡Caramba!; ¡Carambita! [SP]

Other useful vocabulary – Vocabulario útil suplementario

Yes. – Sí.

No. – No.

I am... – soy...

he is... – el es...

you are... – eres...*(informal)*; usted es...*(formal)*

my friend is... – un amigo mío es... *(male friend)*/una amiga mía es... *(female friend)*

my friends are... – mis amigos son... *(male friends)*/mis amigas son... *(female*

friends) *(pl. adj.*+ -s)
my boyfriend is... – mi pareja/amigo/novio es...
adult – adulto
AIDS – SIDA
bent [UK]; homo [US] – invertido; maricón; marica; torcido; loca; voltiado [L.AM]; joto [MEX]
bisexual – bisexual
a bitch – una puta; una zorra; una prostituta
to bitch – cotillear; criticar; chismosear
bitchy – cotilla; criticón *(of a man)*/criticona *(of a woman)*; perra; chismosa
body-building – culturismo [SP]; físico-culturista [L.AM]
butch – macho; viril; hombruna *(of a woman)*
camp – maricona; afeminado; loca *(overly camp)*; tener plumero/plumas [SP]
to chat someone up – enrollarse con alguien; ligar; ligarse a alguien; levantarse a alguien [L.AM]
to be 'in the closet' – estar reprimido; esconderse; aislarse
come; spunk – leche; semen
to come – venir; echar leche; correrse [SP]; acabarse [L.AM]; venirse [L.AM]
to 'come out' – liberarse; destaparse
a cow – una estirada; una creída; una foca [SP]
to cruise – ligar; vacilar; levantar
drag – vestido de travesti; travestido; vestido de mujer
drag shows – espectáculos de travestís
a dyke [UK]; a lesbo [US] – una tortillera [SP]; una bollera [SP]; una torta [L.AM]; una arepera [L.AM]
a butch dyke – una camionera; una machorra
erect – erecto; duro; empalmado [SP]; envergado [L.AM]; parado [L.AM]
an erection; a hard-on – una erección; estar empalmado *(to have a hard-on)*; estar envergado [L.AM]*(to have a hard-on)*
a fag hag – una chica que siempre va con gays; una jotera [MEX]
female – femenino
french-kissing – besos a la francesa; besos franceses; un morreo [SP]
a fuck – un polvo; echar un polvo *(to have a fuck)*
gay – gai; gay; homosexual; maricón; marica; mariquita; loca ; joto [MEX]
the gay scene – el ambiente gay; el escenario gay
a girl – una chica; una muchacha

a guy – un tipo; un muchacho; un chico; torcido; un tío [SP]

the leather scene – el ambiente de (ropa de) cuero

a lesbian – una lesbiana

male – masculino

men only – sólo para hombres

the nightclub – el nightclub

the nudist beach – la playa nudista

to pick someone up – llevarse a alguien a casa; tirarse a alguien; ligarse a alguien

to be pissed off with someone – estar cansado/mamado [L.AM] de alguien; ester mosqueado/cabreado con alguien [SP]

a poof; a faggot [US] – un maricón; un joto [MEX]

a queen – una reina; una marica; una loca; una plumera [SP]; una plumífera [SP]; un voltiado [L.AM]

queer – marica; – moña [MEX]

queer-bashing – atacar a homosexuales

a rent boy – un prostituto; un chapero [SP]; un taxi-boy [L.AM]

SM (sadomasochism) – masoca *(adj)*; sadomasoquismo; los masocas *(people who practice S&M)*

skinheads – skinheads; cabezas rapadas; pelados; calvos

a slut – una marrana; un putón; un pendón; una pendona; un puto

straight – hetero; heterosexual; no brinca [L.AM]; buga [MEX]

a tart – una puta; una fulana; una ramera; un puto; un vendido

a transvestite – un travestí; un transvestido; una loca [L.AM]

a wank – una paja; un rapidito [MEX]; una chaqueta [MEX]

women only – sólo para mujeres

one – uno

two – dos

three – tres

four – cuatro

five – cinco

six – seis

seven – siete

eight – ocho

nine – nueve

ten – diez

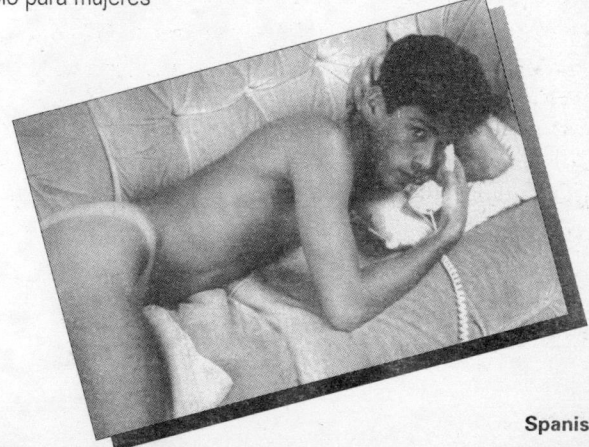

eleven – once
twelve – doce
thirteen – trece
fourteen – catorce
fifteen – quince
sixteen – dieciséis
seventeen – diecisiete
eighteen – dieciocho
nineteen – diecinueve
twenty – veinte
twenty one – veintiuno
twenty two – veintidós
thirty – treinta
thirty one – treinta y uno
thirty two – treinta y dos
forty – cuarenta
fifty – cincuenta
sixty – sesenta
seventy – setenta
eighty – ochenta

ninety – noventa
one hundred – cien/ciento
two hundred – doscientos
three hundred – trescientos
four hundred – cuatrocientos
five hundred – quinientos
six hundred – seiscientos
seven hundred – setecientos
eight hundred – ochocientos
nine hundred – novecientos
one thousand – mil

Talking safer sex!

In the hotel lobby – En la recepción del hotel

Hello! Do you have any single rooms?
¡Hola! ¿Tienen habitaciones individuales?

No, I'm afraid not. But we do have a bed in a twin room if you don't mind sharing.
Lo siento pero no tenemos, pero lo que sí tenemos es una cama libre en una habitación compartida, si no le importa.

That's fine.
De acuerdo.

Well it's room 69, the other guy has just checked in.
Muy bien. Es la 69, el otro ocupante acaba de llegar.

Thanks.
Gracias.

(Upstairs...
En la habitatión...)

Hi!
¡Hola!

- **Hello!**
- ¿Qué tal?

Just arrived?
¿Acabas de llegar?

- **Yeah.**
- Sí.

Where are you from?
¿De dónde eres?

- **London. You?**
- De Londres. ¿Y tú?

New York.
De Nueva York.

- **Have you been here before?**
- ¿Ya has estado aquí antes?

Yes. A couple of times.
Sí. Un par de veces.

- **Do you know any good bars?**
- ¿Conoces algunos bares que estén bien?

Yes sure, I'll give you a tour later. Just let me grab a shower.
Sí, ¿cómo no? Después te llevo a dar una vuelta, pero antes tengo que ducharme.

(A few minutes later...
Unos minutos después...)

Can you pass me the shampoo?
¿Me pasas el champú, por favor?

- **Yeah sure - here you are.**
- Sí, hombre, aquí tienes.

Why don't you come in and join me?
¿Por qué no te metes en la ducha conmigo?

- **OK!**
- ¡Vale!

That's good, I love that!
¡Oh, sí, me gusta!

- **Well, turn around and let me do your front. Oh! You are enjoying it, aren't you? Let me take care of that.**
- Ahora gírate que te frotaré por delante. ¡Ah! Te gusta, ¿eh? Deja que me encargue de eso.

Wow! That's wonderful.
¡Uau! ¡Es tope!

- **Let's get out of here and find some condoms. I want you to fuck me.**
- Vamos a por condones. Quiero que me folles.

Did you bring any condoms?
¿Has traído condones?

- **No, I was hoping you'd have some.**
- No, creía que tú lleverías.

Well, let's do it anyway.
Bueno, no importa. Te follo igualmente.

- **No way! Let's stay in here for a bit while I take care of your dick. You can't beat a blow job in the shower and we'll go and find some condoms for later.**
- ¡Ni hablar! Nos quedamos aquí mientras yo me encargo de tu polla. No me dirás que no a una mamada bajo la ducha, ¿verdad? Después ya iremos a por condones.

Suits me!
¡Vale!

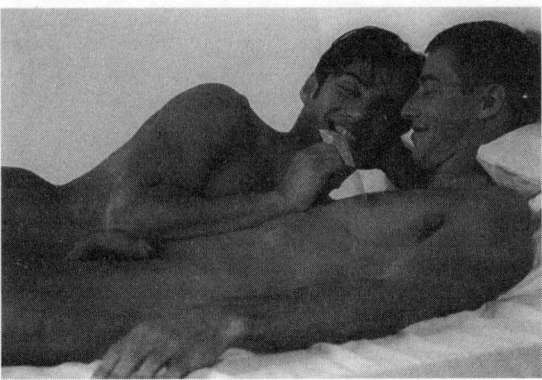

ITALIAN

The Bar/Club – Il Bar/il Club

I would like ... please. – Vorrei ... per favore; Mi porti ... per favore.
- **a half-pint [UK]** – una birra piccola; una mezza birra
- **a pint [UK]** – una birra media
- **a beer** – una birra
- **a light beer** – una birra leggera
- **a heavy beer [UK]** – una birra scura
- **a shandy [UK]** – una birra e gassosa
- **a glass of red wine** – un bicchiere di vino rosso
- **a glass of white wine** – un bicchiere di vino bianco
- **a gin and tonic** – un gin e tonica
- **a vodka** – una vodka
- **a vodka and coke/orange** – una vodka e coca/una vodka con succo d'arancia; una vodka all'arancia; una vodka con spremuta
- **a whisky; a scotch [US]** – un whisky
- **a rum** – un rum
- **a cider** – un sidro
- **a coke** – una coca
- **a lemonade** – una gassosa; una limonata
- **an orange juice** – un succo d'arancia; una spremuta
- **an apple juice** – un succo di mela
- **a mineral water** – una acqua minerale
- **a coffee** – un caffè
- **white coffee** – caffè con latte; un caffè macchiato
- **a tea** – un tè
- **hot/cold milk** – latte caldo/freddo
- **a hot chocolate** – una cioccolata calda

with/without – con.../senza...
- **sugar** – zucchero
- **milk** – latte
- **ice** – ghiaccio
- **water** – acqua
- **soda** – soda
- **tonic** – tonica
- **blackcurrant** – succo di more nere
- **lemon juice** – succo di limone

How much is that? – Quanto viene?; Quanto costa?

Is this seat free? – È libero questo posto?
- **Yes (it's free).** – Sì (è libero).
- **No (it's taken).** – No (è occupato).

Where are the toilets? – Dove sono i bagni?
- **at the back** – dietro
- **on the right** – sulla destra
- **on the left** – sulla sinistra

downstairs – da basso; di sotto; giú
upstairs – di sopra

Do you sell anything to eat? – Ha qualcosa da mangiare?

something hot/cold – qualcosa di caldo/freddo

Have you got a menu? – Avete un menú?

Do you sell...? – Vendete...?
matches – fiammiferi
cigarettes – sigarette
poppers – dei popper
condoms; rubbers [US] – dei condom; dei preservativi
lubricant – lubrificante

What time does this place close/open? – A che ora chiude/apre questo posto?

At...o'clock – Alle...
at one o'clock – all'una
two – due
three – tre
four – quattro
five – cinque
six – sei
seven – sette
eight – otto
nine – nove
ten – dieci
eleven – undici
twelve – dodici
half past one – l'una e mezza
half past two – le due e mezza

Cruising – Battuage

Hi! – Ciao!

Hello! – Ciao!; Salve!

Good evening. – Buona sera.

How are you? – Come stai?; Come va?
good – bene
OK – non c'è male; così così

Do you speak... – Parli...
English – l'inglese
French – il francese
German – il tedesco
Italian – l'italiano
Spanish – lo spagnolo
Dutch – l'olandese
Portuguese – il portoghese

Yes (I speak ...). – Sì (parlo...).
a bit – un po'

No (I don't speak...). – No (non parlo...).

I'm sorry, I don't speak... – Mi dispiace, non parlo...

I don't understand. – Non capisco.

Can you repeat that (please)? – Puoi ripetere (per favore)? *(informal)*; Può ripetere (per favore)? *(formal)*

Can you speak more slowly please? – Puoi parlare più lentamente? *(informal)*; Può parlare più lentamente? *(formal)*

Have you got a light? – Hai d'accendere?

Have you got the time? – Può dire l'ora?

Thank you! – Grazie!

Are you on your own? – Sei da solo?

I'm with my boyfriend. – Sono con il mio ragazzo.

I'm with my friend/friends. – Sono con il mio amico. *(male friend)*; Sono con la mia amica. *(female friend)* / Sono con i miei amici.

What's your name? – Come ti chiami?

My name is... – Mi chiamo...

Where do you come from? – Da dove vieni?

I come... – Vengo...
    from England – dall'Inghilterra
    from Scotland – dalla Scozia
    from Wales – dal Galles
    from Britain – dalla Gran Bretagna
    from Ireland – dall'Irlanda
    from France – dalla Francia
    from Germany – dalla Germania
    from Spain – dalla Spagna
    from Portugal – dal Portogallo
    from Italy – dall'Italia
    from Switzerland – dalla Svizzera
    from Belgium – dal Belgio
    from Austria – dall'Austria
    from Holland – dall'Olanda; dai Paesi Bassi
    from the United States – dagli Stati Uniti; dall'America
    from Canada – dal Canada
    from Japan – dal Giappone
    from Australia – dall'Australia
    from New Zealand – dalla Nuova Zelanda

Do you come here often? – Vieni spesso qui?

Would you like ...? – Vuoi...?
    a drink – una bibita
    a cigarette – una sigaretta

(No, thank you) I don't smoke. – (No, grazie) non fumo.

Are you on holiday [UK]/vacation [US]? – Sei in vacanza?
    Yes (I'm on holiday [UK]/vacation [US]). – Sì (sono in vacanza).
    (No) I work here. – (No) lavoro qui.
    I study here. – Studio qui.

Where do you live? – Dove abiti?
Where are you staying? – Dove stai?
I live... – Abito…
I'm staying... – Sto…
  with friends – con amici
  in a hotel – in un albergo
  in a flat [UK]/apartment [US]
    – in un appartamento
  in a house – in una casa

Would you like to go …?
  – Vorresti andare…?
  to a cafe – in un caffè bar
  to a restaurant – in un ristorante
  to another bar – in un altro bar/pub
  to a disco – in una discoteca
  to a sauna – in una sauna
  to the beach – alla spiaggia
  to the pool – alla piscina
  for a walk – per una passeggiata

Would you like to … with me?
  – Vorresti … con me?
  dance – ballare
  have a drink – bere qualcosa
  have something to eat – mangiare

Can I buy you a drink?
  – Posso offrirti una bevanda?

What would you like (to drink)?
  – Cosa gradisci (da bere)?

It's … here tonight, (isn't it?)
  – È … qui stanotte (non è vero)?
  packed – pienissimo
  busy – affollato; animato
  dead – morto
  boring – noioso

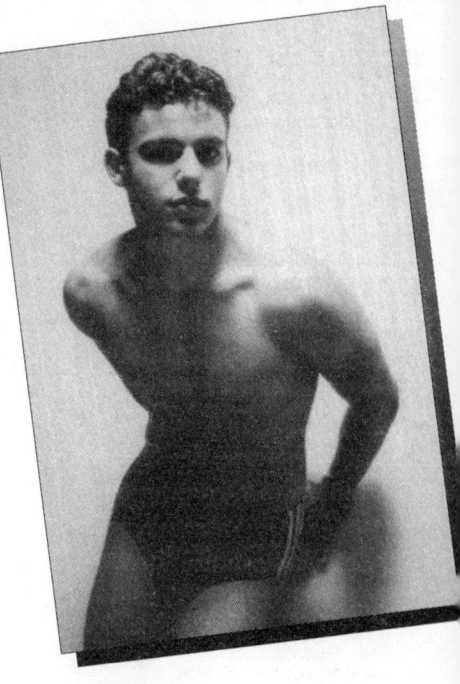

I like your... – mi piace…
  jacket – la tua giacca
  shirt – la tua camicia
  I like your clothes. – Mi piacciono i tuoi vestiti.
  I like your haircut. – Mi piace il taglio dei capelli.

Where did you get it/them from? – Dove l'hai presa?/Dove li hai presi?
Where did you get your hair done? – Dove li hai tagliati i capelli?
You look very smart/nice tonight! – Stai proprio bene stasera!/Sei proprio bello stasera!
How old are you? – Quanti anni hai?
I'm ... (years old). – Ho … anni.
(see numbers on page 74)

Nice eyes! – Che begl'occhi!
Nice legs! – Che belle gambe!
Nice bum! – Che culo!
What a nice smile you have! – Hai un bel sorriso!
You're... – Sei...
    beautiful – molto bello
    handsome – molto bello; figo; di bell' aspetto; benfatto
    hunky – molto bono; figo
    a hunk – un fusto; un figo
    gorgeous – bellissimo; molto affascinante; molto attraente; splendido; magnifico
    sweet – molto dolce
    cute – carino
    sexy – molto sexy
    attractive – molto attraente
You really turn me on. – Mi sconvolgi!; Mi fai (ribollire il) sangue!
You really make me hot. – Mi fai impazzire!
I'm crazy about you. – Sono pazzo di te!
You're not my type. – Non sei il mio tipo.
I'm not interested. – Non mi interessi.
Get lost! – Togliti dai piedi!; Va al diavolo!
Piss off! – Va a cagare!
What type of guys do you like? – Che tipo di ragazzo ti piace?
What are you into? – Cosa ti piace?; Cosa ti interessa?
I'm into... *(plural nouns)* Mi interessano...; Mi piacciono...
I'm not into...; I don't like... *(plural nouns)* – Non mi interessano...;
    Non mi piacciono...
    older men – gli uomini maturi
    younger men – i giovani
    blonde guys – i biondi
    guys with brown hair – i castani
    guys with dark hair – i bruni
    red heads – uomini con i capelli rossi
    guys with short hair – uomini con i capelli corti
    guys with long hair – uomini con i capelli lunghi
    hunky guys; well-built guys – i fusti
    thin guys – i magri
    chubby guys – i robusti
    tall guys – gli uomini alti
    short guys – gli uomini bassi
    guys with dark eyes – uomini con gli occhi scuri
    guys with blue eyes – uomini con gli occhi azzurri
    dildos – i dildo
    tatoos – i tatuaggi
    boots – i stivali
    uniforms – le divise

I'm into... *(singular nouns)* – Mi interessa...; Mi piace...

I'm not into...,I don't like...*(singular nouns)* – Non mi interessa...; Non mi piace...
- **denim** – il denim
- **leather** – il leather; la pelle; vestiti di cuoio
- **rubber** – la gomma
- **water sports** – il pissing
- **fisting** – il fist fucking
- **threesomes** – fare il triangolo
- **cross-dressing** – travestirmi
- **piercing** – farmi forare
- **brown; scat** – lo scatto
- **bondage** – farmi legare *(you to me)*; farti legare *(me to you)*; il bondage

Is there somewhere quieter/more private we can go? – C'e una parte più calma/più privata dove si può stare?

Do you want to come to my place? – Vuoi venire a casa mia?

Yes. – Sì.

I'm sorry, I can't. – Mi dispiace, non posso.

Can we meet again? – Ci possiamo incontrare ancora?

When? – Quando?

Would you like to meet me...? – Ti piacerebbe incontrarmi...?
- **this evening** – questa sera
- **tomorrow** – domani
- **tomorrow morning** – domani mattina
- **tomorrow afternoon** – domani pomeriggio
- **tomorrow night** – domani sera
- **on Monday** – lunedì
- **on Tuesday** – martedì
- **on Wednesday** – mercoledì
- **on Thursday** – giovedì
- **on Friday** – venerdì
- **on Saturday** – sabato
- **on Sunday** – domenica

At what time? – A che ora?

At ... o'clock – Alle...; All'una *(at one o'clock)* (see page 60)

Where? – Dove?
- **here** – qui
- **at my hotel** – al mio albergo
- **at my flat [UK]/apartment [US]** – al mio appartamento
- **at my house** – alla mia casa
- **at my friend's place** – dal mio amico
- **at your place** – a casa tua

Can I have your phone number? – Posso avere il tuo numero di telefono?

Can I have your address? – Posso avere il tuo indirizzo?

Bye. – Ciao!

Goodbye. – Arrivederci!   **See you again!** – Ci vediamo!

At his place/your place – A casa sua/a casa tua

Would you like some...? – Vuoi del...?
- **coffee** – caffè
- **tea** – tè
- **wine** – vino
- **orange juice** – succo d'arancia

Would you like something to eat? – Vuoi qualcosa da mangiare?

Are you hungry/thirsty? – Hai fame/sete?

Are you cold/too hot? – Hai freddo/troppo caldo?

Do you want to watch TV/a video? – Vuoi guardare la TV/un video?

Would you like to listen to some music? – Vorresti ascoltare un po' di musica?

What kind of music do you like? – Che tipo di musica ti piace?
- **classical** – musica classica
- **opera** – opera
- **jazz** – jazz
- **rock** – rock
- **pop** – pop
- **folk** – folk
- **traditional** – tradizionale

Can I kiss you? – Posso darti un bacio?

Would you like...? – Vorresti...?
- **a massage** – un massaggio
- **a blow job** – un pompino

What do you like doing? – Cosa ti piace fare?

I like... – Mi piace...

I don't like... – Non mi piace...

Do you like...? – Ti piace...?
- **kissing** – baciare
- **cuddling** – coccolare
- **fucking** – scopare; chiavare
- **being fucked** – essere scopato; essere chiavato
- **sucking** – succhiare
- **being sucked** – farmelo succhiare
- **wanking; jerking off [US]** – masturbare; farmi una sega *(alone)*; farti una sega *(me to you)*
- **mutual masturbation** – la masturbazione reciproca; farci una reciproca sega
- **licking** – leccare
- **stroking** – accarezzare
- **rubbing** – pomiciare
- **spanking** – sculacciare; schiaffeggiare
- **being spanked** – essere sculacciato
- **cross-dressing** – travestirmi; *(Do you like...? Ti piace travestirti?)*
- **shaving** – rasare
- **fisting** – il fist fucking
- **rimming** – leccare il culo

Are you..?/I am ... – Sei...?/Sono...

experienced – esperto
inexperienced – inesperto

I like to be... – Preferisco essere...
  active – attivo
  passive – passivo

Shall we go to the bedroom/bathroom? – Andiamo a letto/in bagno?

Have you got any...? – Hai dei...?
  condoms; rubbers [US] – condom; preservativi; profilattici
  toys – giocattoli erotici/sensuali
  lubricant – lubrificante
  poppers – popper

Are you into safer sex? – Fai del sesso sicuro?; Pratichi sesso sicuro?

I'm only into safer sex. – Faccio solo del sesso sicuro; Pratico solo sesso sicuro.

I'm HIV-positive. – Sono sieropositivo.

Are you HIV-positive? – Sei sieropositivo?

Would you like a shower (with me)? – Vorresti fare una doccia (con me)?

Take off your...! – Levati...!;Togliti...!

Take off your clothes! – Spogliati!

Can I take off your...? – Posso levarti...?: Posso toglierti...?; Posso spogliati? *(Can I take off your clothes?)*
  clothes – i vestiti
  shirt – la camicia
  trousers; pants [US] – i pantaloni
  socks – le calze
  briefs; underpants; shorts [US] – lo slip; le mutande; il boxer

Lie down! – Sdraiati!

Bend over! – Chinati!

Sit down! – Siediti!

You're really nice. – Sei proprio carino.

I like...(singular nouns) – Mi piace ...

Can I kiss...? – Posso baciare...?

Can I suck...? – Posso succhiare...?

Can I touch...? – Posso toccare...?

Can I feel...? – Posso accarezzare...?
  your cock – il tuo cazzo; il tuo uccello; il tuo pisello
  your bum – il tuo culo
  your body – il tuo corpo
  your figure – il tuo aspetto
  your (hairy) chest – il tuo petto (peloso)
  your toe – il tuo alluce

I like your ... (plural nouns) – Mi piacciono...
  your balls – le tue palle; i tuoi coglioni

your nipples – i tuoi capezzoli
your legs – le tue gambe

That feels good! – Mi piace!; Mi stravolgi!
That's great! – Bello!
That's wonderful! – Magnifico!
That's really good! – È proprio bello!
Do that again! – (Fallo) ancora!
My god, that's wonderful! – Madonna/Mamma mia, è magnifico!
Yes...yes... – Sì..., sì...
Come on! – Dai!
Fuck me! – Scopami!; Chiavami!
Suck me! – Succhiami!
Wank me! – Fammi una sega!
Spank me! – Sculacciami!; Schiaffeggiami!
Harder, harder! – Più forte, più forte!
Slower, slower! – Lento, lento!
I'm coming...! – Sto venendo...!
Come all over me! – Vienimi a dosso!
I don't like that! – Non mi piace!
Stop! – Basta!; Fermati!
That hurts! – Mi fa male!
Not so fast/hard! – No così veloce/forte!
Don't come in my mouth/arse! – Non venire nella mia bocca!/ Non venire nel mio culo!
That was wonderful. – È stato bello.
Would you like to clean yourself up? – Vorresti pulirti?
Have you got any tissues/ a towel? – Hai fazzolettini/un asciugamano?
Here you are! – Eccolo!
May I use your shower? – Posso usare la tua doccia?
Shall we have a shower together? – Facciamo una doccia insieme?
Can I have a towel (please)? – Posso avere una asciugamano (per favore)?
Good night! – Buona notte!
Sleep well! – Dormi bene!
I love you. – Ti amo.
Did you sleep well? – Hai dormito bene?
I'll have to ask you to leave now. – Potresti andare via.

Italian 67

Can you go now please? – Se puoi andare per favore.
I have to go now. – Devo andare.
Would you like some breakfast? – Vorresti fare prima colazione?
Can I write to you? – Posso scriverti?
It's been nice knowing you! – È stato bello conoscerti!
Would you like to see me again? – Se ti piacerebbe rivedermi?
Can I see you again? – Posso rivederti?
Goodbye! – Ciao!
See you again! – Ci vediamo!; Arrivederci!
Take care. – Prenditi cura; Stai bene.

On the telephone – Al telefono

Hello! – Pronto!
Can I speak with ... (please)? – Posso parlare con ... (per favore)?
Hang on... – Un momento...; Aspetti...
...speaking! – sono...
It's me! – Sono io!
It's ... – È...
I'm phoning you as we arranged. – Ti chiamo come abbiamo programmato.
Can we meet ... – Possiamo incontrarci...
    this evening – questa sera
    at... o'clock – alle...; all'una *(at one o'clock) (see page 60)*
Where? – Dove?
At... – A...; Al...; Alla...
Can you spell it? – Puoi fare lo spelling?
OK, thank you! – OK, grazie!
See you later! – Ci vediamo più tardi!
He is not here! – Lui non è qui!
Can you phone again... – Puoi richiamare di nuovo...
    later – più tardi
    this afternoon – questo pomeriggio
I don't understand. – Non capisco.
Do you speak...? – Parla...? *(formal)*; Parli...? *(informal)*
Please speak slowly. – Parli lentamente per favore. *(formal)*;
    Parla lentamente per favore. *(informal)*

Health – La salute

I need to see a doctor. – Mi serve un dottore/medico.
doctor – dottore; medico
surgery [UK]; doctor's office [US] – chirurgia
chemist [UK]; pharmacy – la farmacia
I have... – Ho...
I have caught... – Ho preso...
I think I have... – Penso di avere...
Do you have something for...? – Ha qualcosa contro...
  gonorrhoea – la gonorrea; lo scolo
  syphilis – la sifilide
  crabs – le piattole
  lice – i pidocchi
  herpes – l'herpes
  scabies – la scabbia
I hurt here. – Mi fa male qui.
I'm bleeding. – Sto perdendo sangue.
I'm itching. – Io prudo.
My throat/penis/anus hurts. – La gola/il pene/l'ano mi fa male.

Services – Servizi

Can you help me? – Può aiutarmi? (formal); Puoi aiutarmi? (informal)
How much is this/that? – Quanto costa questo/questa?
Have you got a map of...? – Hai una mappa di/cartina di...?
Have you got a map of the city? – Hai una mappa di/cartina della città?
Can I have the number for Gay Switchboard? – Posso avere il numero del centro d'informazione gay?
Can I have the number of the AIDS helpline? – Posso avere il numero della linea telefonica del'aiuto per l'AIDS?
Can you give me the name of a doctor who is experienced in AIDS/HIV-related problems? – Può darmi il nome di un dottore specializzato in problemi relativi all'AIDS/del sieropositivitá?
Can you give me the name of a clinic which is experienced in AIDS/HIV-related problems? – Può darmi il nome di una clinica specializzata in problemi relativi all'AIDS/del sieropositivitá?
Can you give me the name of a gay- friendly doctor? – Può darmi il nome di un dottore alla mano con i gay?

Excuse me! – Scusa

Where is/are...? – Dovè.../Dove sono...
   the sauna – la sauna
   the cruising areas – i posti dove si batte; le zone di battuage
   the gay bars – i bar gay
   the cottages [UK]; tea rooms [US] – i diurni
   the gay bookshop – la libreria gay
   the gay hotels – gli alberghi gay

Contact ads – Segnalazioni

I am... – Sono...

I am looking for a ... guy – Cerco un ragazzo...
   active – attivo
   affectionate – affettuoso
   athletic – atletico
   attractive – attraente
   bisexual – bisessuale
   boyish – puerile; fanciullesco
   caring – affettuoso; bonario
   Christian – cristiano
   chubby – robusto; grassottello
   clean – pulito
   clean-shaven – senza barba o baffi
   conservative – conservatore
   considerate – gentile
   cuddly – coccolone; accarazzaribile
   cute – carino
   discreet – discreto
   dominant – dominante
   easy-going – senza complessi
   educated – educato; colto;
       di buona cultura; istruito
   experienced – esperto
   friendly – simpatico; socievole
   gentle – gentile; tenero
   good-looking – piacente; di bella presenza
   hairy – peloso; villoso
   handsome – molto bello; figo; di bell' aspetto; benfatto
   honest – onesto
   horny – arrapato
   with a good sense of humour – con un buon senso dell'umorismo (*I have a good sense of humour* Ho un buon senso dell'umorismo)
   independent – indipendente
   inexperienced – inesperto
   intelligent – intelligente
   interesting – interessante
   introverted – introverso
   lonely – solitario; solo
   loyal – leale; fedele
   married – sposato
   masculine – maschio; virile
   mature – maturo

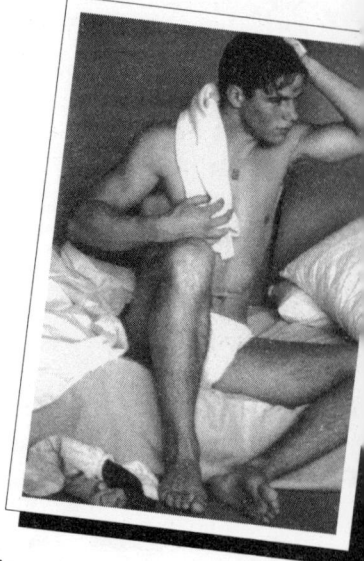

of medium build – di statura normale
middle aged – di mezza età
military – militare; in divisa *(in uniform)*
muscular – muscoloso
a nature lover – amante di natura *(used with: I am…)*; amante della natura *(used with: I am looking for…)*
non-scene – fuori ambiente; fuori dal giro; estraneo ambienti
(a) non-smoker – (un) non fumatore
older – più vecchio
open – libero
open minded – liberale; aperto di mente
outgoing – estroverso
passionate – apassionato
passive – passivo
quiet – tranquillo; sereno
radical – radicale
refined – raffinato; delicato; di buona cultura; distinto
reliable – fidato
reserved – riservato
romantic – romantico
of the same age – coetaneo
sensitive – sensibile; delicato; tenero
serious – serio
shy – timido
sincere – sincero; schietto
slim – magro; snello
(a) smoker – (un) fumatore
smooth – glabro; non peloso
special – speciale
spontaneous – spontaneo
sporty – sportivo
straight acting – ineffeminato; insospettabile
straight forward – senza problemi; franco
(a) student – (uno) studente
submissive – sottomesso
tall – alto
transsexual – transessuale
(a) university graduate – (un) laureato
(a) virgin – (un) vergine
warm – affettuoso; caldo
well-endowed; well-hung – (ben) dotato; ben fornito
well-built – ben fatto; robusto
young – giovane
younger – più giovane
youthful – giovanile; efebico

no effeminates – no effeminati; niente effeminati; effeminati astenersi

no fats – no grassi; niente grassi; grassi astenersi

…welcome – ….graditi *(with plurals)*; …gradito *(with singular nouns)*

for friendship – per (una) amicizia

for a relationship – per (una) relazione

for sex – per sesso

...only – solo...

I have... – Ho...
    blue eyes – gli occhi azzurri
    brown eyes – gli occhi castani
    green eyes – gli occhi verdi
    grey eyes – gli occhi grigi
    blonde hair – i capelli biondi
    brown hair – i capelli castani
    black hair – i capelli neri
    red hair – i capelli rossi
    grey hair – i capelli grigi
    dark hair – i capelli bruni
    short hair – i capelli corti
    long hair – i capelli lunghi

I have a beard.
    – Io ho la barba.

I have a moustache.
    – Io ho i baffi.

I'm bald. – Sono calvo.

Expressions – Espressioni

My God! – Madonna!; Mamma mia!; Dio mio!

Fantastic! – Fantastico!

I'm sorry. – Mi dispiace.

Excuse me! – Scusami!

Get fucked! – Fottiti!

Fuck off! – Vaffanculo!

Shit! – Merda!

Darling! – Caro!

My dear! – Caro mio!

Honey! – Tesoro!; Gioia!; Zucchero!

Oh dear! – O caro!

How wonderful! – Che bello!; Stupendo!

How awful! – Bruttissimo!; Che schifo!

He's a friend of Dorothy. – È una checca; È frocio.

As camp as knickers. – Che frocio.

Wow! – Uao!; Hippa!; Che fuoco!

Other useful vocabulary – Altri vocabolario utili

Yes – Sì
No – No
I am... – sono...
he is... – lui è...
you are... – tu sei... *(informal)*; lei è... *(formal)*
my friend is... – il mio amico è...
my friends are... – i miei amici sono... *(adj + -i/e)*
my boyfriend is... – il mio ragazzo è...
adult – adulto
AIDS – AIDS
bent [UK]; homo [US] – invertito
bisexual – bisessuale
a bitch – una puttana
to bitch – sparlare; pettegolare; parlar male
bitchy – pettegolo; malèvolo
body-building – culturismo
butch – macho
camp – effeminato
to chat someone up – sollecitare qualcuno al contatto
to be 'in the closet' – nascondersi; tenerlo per sé
come; spunk – la sborra
to come – venire; giungere; sborrare
to 'come out' – venir fuori; quando mi sono scoperto e accettato
a cow – una vacca; una vaccona
to cruise – battere
drag – travestitismo
drag shows – spettacoli di travestiti
a dyke [UK]; a lesbo [US] – una lesbica
a butch dyke – una camionista
erect – eretto
an erection; a hard-on – una erezione
a fag hag – una donna da froci; una strega da froci
female – femmina
french-kissing – bacio profondo

a fuck – una scopata
gay – gay; omosessuale
the gay scene – l'ambiente gay; la vita gay
a girl – una ragazza
a guy – un ragazzo
the leather scene – l'ambiente leather
a lesbian – una lesbica
male – maschio
men only – solo uomini
the nightclub – il night
the nudist beach – la spiaggia nudista
to pick someone up – rimorchiare qualcuno; beccare qualcuno
to be pissed off with someone – essere seccato con qualcuno
a poof; a faggot [US] – un frocio; un finocchio
a queen – una checca; una dama; una prima donna
queer – rotto in culo (*adj*); finocchio
queer-bashing – picchiatori di froci
a rent-boy – un ragazzo che marchetta
SM (sadomasochism) – sadomasochismo
skinheads – skinheads
a slut – una zoccola
straight – étero
a tart – una troia
a transvestite – un travestito
a wank – una sega
women only – solo donne

one – uno
two – due
three – tre
four – quattro
five – cinque
six – sei
seven – sette
eight – otto
nine – nove
ten – dieci
eleven – undici
twelve – dodici
thirteen – tredici
fourteen – quattordici
fifteen – quindici
sixteen – sedici
seventeen – diciassette
eighteen – diciotto
nineteen – dicianove
twenty – venti
twenty one – ventuno
twenty two – ventidue
thirty – trenta
forty – quaranta
fifty – cinquanta
sixty – sessanta
seventy – settanta
eighty – ottanta
ninety – novanta
one hundred – cento
one thousand – mille

Talking safer sex!

On the beach – Nella spiaggia

Hi! Nice tan you've got there!
Ciao! Che bella abbronzatura che hai!

Thanks, yours is pretty good.
Grazie, la tua non è male.

Have you been here long?
Sei qui da molto?

A couple of hours.
Un paio di ore.

Do you fancy a walk...in the dunes?
Ti va di fare una passeggiata...fra le rovine?

Yeah, sure!
Sì, certamente!

(Later in the dunes...
Più tardi alle rovine...)

Shall we sit here for a bit?
Ci sediamo per un pò qui?

OK.
Va bene.

Have you got a boyfriend?
Hai un amante?

Yeah, he's gone back to the hotel with a blonde German!
Sì, ma è andato in albergo con un ragazzo biondo tedesco!

Oh, I see. You're not into monogamy then?
O capisco, non sei un tipo monotono.

No way!
Certamente no!

That's good, come here...
Va bene, vieni qui...

Mmmm, that feels good!
Mmmm, cosí mi piace!

I'd love to suck your dick.
Mi piacerebbe succhiarti il cazzo.

Do you mind if I wear a condom?
Ti dispiace se metto il preservativo?

I'd rather you didn't, I can't stand the taste.
Preferirei di no! Non sopporto il gusto.

Here, I've got some chocolate flavoured ones.
Qui, ho un po' alla cioccolata.

Go on then!
Va bene!

Oh god! That's good!
O dio, mi piace!

I'd love you to fuck me.
Vorrei che mi scopassi.

I don't fuck except with my boyfriend.
Non scopo, tranne che con il mio amante.

Oh well, that's OK, this feels fabulous.
Va bene, cosí è bellissimo.

Don't cum in my mouth!
Non venirmi in bocca!

No, I'm going to cum all over your chest!
No, ma voglio venirti sul torso!

Oh yes!
O sì!

God! I'm coming! Ahhhhh!
Dio! Vengo! Ahhhhh!

Fancy a swim?
Facciamo una nuotata?

Dutch

The Bar/Club – De Bar/Club

I would like ... please – ...alstublieft; Kan je me ... geven?
- **a half-pint [UK]** – een glas bier
- **a pint [UK]** – een groot glas bier
- **a beer** – een bier; een biertje
- **a light beer** – een buckler; een malt; een alcoholvrij bier *(all meaning alcohol free beer)*
- **a heavy beer [UK]** – *(doesn't exist in Holland)*
- **a shandy [UK]** – een sneeuwwitje; een shandy
- **a glass of red wine** – een (glas) rode wijn
- **a glass of white wine** – een (glas) witte wijn
- **a gin and tonic** – een gin en tonic
- **a vodka** – een wodka
- **a vodka and coke/orange** – een wodka-coke/een wodka-sjuutje *or* een wodka-sinaasappelsap
- **a whisky; a scotch [US]** – een whisky
- **a rum** – een rum
- **a cider** – een cider
- **a coke** – een coke
- **a lemonade** – een limonade
- **an orange juice** – een sjuutje; een sinaasappelsap
- **an apple juice** – een appelsap
- **a mineral water** – een mineraal water; een spuitwater
- **a coffee** – een koffie; een kopje koffie
- **white coffee** – koffie met melk
- **a tea** – een thee; een kopje thee
- **hot/cold milk** – warme/koude melk
- **a hot chocolate** – warme chocolade

with/without – met.../zonder...
- **sugar** – suiker
- **milk** – melk
- **ice** – ijs; ijsblokjes
- **water** – water
- **soda** – soda
- **tonic** – tonic
- **blackcurrant** – zwarte bessen; cassis
- **lemon juice** – citroensap

How much is that? – Hoeveel is dat?; Wat krijg je?

Is this seat free? – Is deze plaats vrij?
- **Yes (it's free).** – Ja (hij is vrij).
- **No (it's taken).** – Nee (hij is bezet).

Where are the toilets? – Waar is de W.C.?; Waar zijn de toiletten?
- **at the back** – achterin
- **on the right** – rechts
- **on the left** – links

downstairs – beneden
upstairs – boven

Do you sell anything to eat? – Heb je iets te eten?

something hot/cold – iets warms/iets kouds

Have you got a menu? – Heb je het menu?

Do you sell...? – Heb je...?; Verkoop je...?
matches – lucifers
cigarettes – sigaretten
poppers – poppers
condoms; rubbers [US] – condooms
lubricant – glijmiddel

What time does this place close/open? – Wanneer sluiten/open ze hier?; Hoe laat gaan ze hier dicht/open?

At ... o'clock – Om ... uur
one – één
two – twee
three – drie
four – vier
five – vijf
six – zes
seven – zeven
eight – acht
nine – negen
ten – tien
eleven – elf
twelve – twaalf
half past one – half twee *(in Dutch: half of the following hour)*

Cruising – Cruising

Hi! – Hoi; Hee!

Hello! – Hallo!; Dag!

Good evening. – Goede avond.

How are you? – Hoe gaat het (met je)?
good – goed
OK – OK

Do you speak...? – Spreek je...?
English – Engels
French – Frans
German – Duits
Italian – Italiaans
Spanish – Spaans
Dutch – Nederlands, Vlaams *(Flemish- the Dutch spoken in Belgium)*
Portuguese – Portugees

Yes (I speak ...). – Ja (ik spreek...).
a bit – een beetje

No (I don't speak...). – Nee (ik spreek geen...).

I'm sorry, I don't speak... – Sorry, ik spreek geen...
I don't understand. – Ik begrijp niet (wat je zegt); Ik begrijp het niet.
Can you repeat that (please)? – Kun je dat herhalen? *(informal)*; Kunt u dat herhalen? *(formal)*
Can you speak more slowly please? – Kun je langzamer spreken? *(informal)*; Kunt u langzamer spreken? *(formal)*
Have you got a light? – Heb je een vuurtje?
Have you got the time? – Hoe laat is het?
Thank you! – Bedankt!; Dank je!
Are you on your own? – Ben je alleen?
I'm with my boyfriend. – Ik ben met mijn vriend.
I'm with my friend/friends. – Ik ben met mijn een vriend/vrienden.
What's your name? – Hoe heet je?; Wat is je naam?
My name is... – Ik heet...; Mijn naam is...
Where do you come from? – Waar kom je vandaan?
I come from... – Ik kom uit...
    England – Engeland
    Scotland – Schotland
    Wales – Wales
    Britain – (Groot) Brittannië
    Ireland – Ierland
    France – Frankrijk
    Germany – Duitsland
    Spain – Spanje
    Portugal – Portugal
    Italy – Italië
    Switzerland – Zwitserland
    Belgium – België
    Austria – Oostenrijk
    Holland – Holland, Nederland
    the United States – Amerika; de Verenigde Staten; de U.S.A.
    Canada – Canada
    Japan – Japan
    Australia – Australië
    New Zealand – Nieuw Zeeland
Do you come here often? – Kom je hier vaak?
Would you like ...? – Wil je ...?
    a drink – een drankje; iets drinken
    a cigarette – een sigaret
(No, thank you) I don't smoke. – (Nee, dank je) ik rook niet.
Are you on holiday [UK]/vacation [US]? – Ben je op/met vakantie?
    Yes (I'm on holiday [UK]/vacation [US]). – Ja (ik ben op/met vakantie).
    (No) I work here. – (Nee) ik werk hier.
    I study here. – Ik studeer hier.

Where do you live? – Waar woon je?
Where are you staying? – Waar logeer je?
I live... – Ik woon...
I'm staying... – Ik logeer...
   with friends – bij vrienden
   in a hotel – in een hotel
   in a flat [UK]/apartment [US] – in een flat
   in a house – in een huis

Would you like to go ...? – Heb je zin om ... te gaan?
   to a cafe – naar een café
   to a restaurant – naar een restaurant
   to another bar – naar een andere bar
   to a disco – naar een disco
   to a sauna – naar een sauna
   to the beach – naar het strand
   to the pool – naar het zwembad
   Would you like to go for a walk – Heb je zin om een wandelingetje te maken?; Zullen we een eindje gaan lopen?

Would you like to ... with me? – Wil je met me...?; Heb je zin om met me te...?
   dance – dansen
   have a drink – wil je iets (met me) drinken?
   Would you like to have something to eat with me? – Zullen we samen iets eten?

Can I buy you a drink? – Kan ik je iets te drinken aanbieden?
What would you like (to drink)? – Wat wil je drinken?
It's ... here tonight, (isn't it?) – Het is ... hier vanavond, (niet)?
   packed – stampvol; bomvol
   busy – druk; vol; een gezellige boel
   dead – een dooie boel
   boring – saai

I like your ... – Wat ...
   jacket – een leuk jek; een leuk jak; een leuk jasje
   shirt – een leuk hemd
   clothes – leuke kleren
   I like your haircut – Wat zit je haar leuk.; Je haar zit goed.

Where did you get it/them from? – Waar heb je dat/die vandaan?; Waar heb je dat/die gekocht?
Where did you get your hair done? – Waar heb je haar laten doen?
You look very smart/nice tonight! – Je ziet er goed/leuk uit vanavond!
How old are you? – Hoe oud ben je?
I'm ... (years old) – Ik ben... *(see numbers on page 93)*
Nice eyes! – Mooie ogen!
Nice legs! – Mooie benen!
Nice bum! – Lekkere kont!; Lekker kontje!

What a nice smile you have! – Wat een leuke (glim)lach; Wat (glim)lach je leuk!; Je lacht leuk!

You're... – Je bent...; Ik vind je...
  beautiful – mooi; knap
  handsome – goed uitziend; mooi; knap; Je ziet er goed uit *(You're handsome)*
  hunky – lekker; stevig; flinkgebouwd
  a hunk – een stuk; een stevige kerel
  gorgeous – lekker; fantastisch
  sweet – lief; lekker
  cute – leuk; aardig
  sexy – sexy
  attractive – attractief

You really turn me on. – Ik word geil van je.

You really make me hot. – Ik word helemaal hitsig/geil van je.

I'm crazy about you. – Ik ben helemaal gek op je.

You're not my type. – Je bent niet mijn type.

I'm not interested. – Ik ben niet geinteresseerd.

Get lost! – Ga weg!; Verdwijn!; Get lost!

Piss off! – Piss off!; Donder op!

What type of guys do you like? – Van wat soort van kerels hou je?; Wat voor kerels vind je leuk/lekker?

What are you into? – Waar ben jij in geinteresseerd?

I'm into... – Ik hou van...

I'm not into...; I don't like... – Ik hou niet van...
  older men – oudere mannen
  younger men – jongere kerels; jongens
  blonde guys – mannen met blond haar; blonde mannen
  guys with brown hair – mannen met bruin haar; bruinharige mannen
  guys with dark hair – mannen met donker/zwart haar; donkerharige/zwartharige mannen
  red heads – mannen met rood haar; roodharige mannen
  guys with short hair – mannen met kort haar
  guys with long hair – mannen met lang haar
  hunky guys; well-built guys – goed gebouwde kerels; stevige kerels
  thin guys – slanke kerels
  chubby guys – mollige kerels
  tall guys – grote kerels
  short guys – korte kerels
  guys with dark eyes – mannen met donkere ogen
  guys with blue eyes – mannen met blauwe ogen; blauwogige mannen
  denim – denim
  leather – leer; leder
  rubber – rubber
  dildos – dildos
  water sports – pisseks
  fisting – vuistneuken; fistfucking
  threesomes – triootjes; trioseks
  cross-dressing – travestie

piercing – piercing
tattoos – tatoeages
boots – laarzen
uniforms – uniformen
brown; scat – poepseks
bondage – bondage; vastbinden

Is there somewhere quieter/more private we can go? – Kunnen we ergens heen waar het wat rustiger/meer privé is?

Do you want to come to my place? – Ga je met me mee naar huis?; Wil je met me mee naar huis?

Yes. – Ja.

I'm sorry, I can't. – Sorry, ik kan niet.; Nee, dat gaat niet.

Can we meet again? – Kan ik je weer zien?

When? – Wanneer?

Would you like to meet me...?
– Zullen we elkaar ... ontmoeten?
this evening – vanavond
tomorrow – morgen
tomorrow morning – morgenochtend
tomorrow afternoon – morgenmiddag
tomorrow night – morgenavond
on Monday – op maandag
on Tuesday – op dinsdag
on Wednesday – op woensdag
on Thursday – op donderdag
on Friday – op vrijdag
on Saturday – op zaterdag
on Sunday – op zondag

At what time? – Hoe laat?

At ... o'clock. – Om ... uur. *(see page 78)*

Where? – Waar?
here – hier
at my hotel – in mijn hotel
at my flat [UK]/apartment [US] – in mijn flat
at my house – bij mij (thuis)
at my friend's place – bij mijn vriend
at your place – bij jou (thuis)

Can I have your phone number?
– Wat is je telefoon nummer?

Can I have your address?
– Wat is je adres?

Bye. – Dag!; Doei!

Goodbye. – Tot ziens!

See you again! – See you!; Tot ziens!

At his place/your place – Bij hem thuis/bij jou thuis!

Would you like some...? – Wil je...?
   coffee – koffie
   tea – thee
   wine – wijn
   orange juice – een sjuutje/een sinaasappelsap

Would you like something to eat? – Wil je iets eten?

Are you hungry/thirsty? – Heb je honger/dorst?; Wil je iets eten/drinken?

Are you cold/too hot? – Heb je het koud?/Heb je het te warm?

Do you want to watch TV/a video? – Wil je TV kijken/een video zien?

Would you like to listen to some music? – Wil je wat muziek horen?; Zal ik een muziekje opzetten?

What kind of music do you like? – Van wat voor een soort muziek hou je?
   classical – klassiek
   opera – opera
   jazz – jazz
   rock – rock
   pop – pop
   folk – folk
   traditional – volksmuziek

Can I kiss you? – Kan ik je zoenen?

Would you like...? – Zal ik je ...?
   a massage – een massage geven
   a blow job – afzuigen; pijpen

What do you like doing? – Wat vind je lekker?; Waar hou je van?

I like... – Ik hou van...; Ik vind ... lekker.

I don't like... – Ik hou niet van...; Ik vind ... niet lekker.

Do you like...? – Hou je van...?; Vind je ... lekker?
   kissing – zoenen
   cuddling – vrijen; knuffelen
   fucking – neuken
   sucking – afzuigen; pijpen
   wanking; jerking off [US] – aftrekken
   mutual masturbation – elkaar aftrekken; wederzijds mastuberen
   licking – likken
   stroking – aaien; liefkozen; strelen
   rubbing – wrijven; tegen elkaar aanwrijven
   spanking – spanking; slaan; billekoek
   cross-dressing – travestie
   shaving – scheren
   fisting – vuistneuken; fistfucking
   rimming – kontlikken

I like... – Ik vind het lekker om...

I don't like... – Ik vind het niet lekker om ...

Do you like...? – Hou je er van om ...?; Vind je het lekker om ...?

being fucked – geneukt te worden
being sucked – afgezogen/gepijpt te worden
being spanked – gespankt te worden; geslagen te worden

Are you...?/I am... – Ben jij...?; Ik ben...
experienced – ervaren
inexperienced – onervaren

I like to be... – Ik ben liever...
active – actief
passive – passief

Shall we go to the bedroom/bathroom? – Zullen we naar bed/in bad gaan?

Have you got any...? – Heb je...?
condoms; rubbers [US] – condooms
toys – toys; speelgoed
lubricant – glijmiddel
poppers – poppers

Are you into safer sex? – Ga je voor veilige/safer sex?; Wil je veilige/safer sex?

I'm only into safer sex. – Ik doe alleen aan veilige/safer sex.

I'm HIV-positive. – Ik ben seropositief.

Are you HIV-positive? – Ben jij seropositief?

Would you like a shower (with me)? – Wil je een douche (met me)?; Wil je onder de douche (met me)?

Take off your...! – Doe je ... uit!

Can I take off your...? – Kan ik je ... uitdoen?

Can I take off your clothes? – Kan ik je uitkleden?
clothes – kleren
shirt – shirt; overhemd
trousers; pants [US] – broek
socks – sokken
briefs; underpants; shorts [US] – slip; onderbroek; shorts

Lie down! – Ga liggen!

Bend over! – Buig je!

Sit down! – Ga zitten!

You're really nice. – Je bent erg aardig.

I like your... – Je hebt ...
cock – een lekkere lul; een lekkere pik
balls – lekkere ballen
bum – lekkere billen; een lekkere kont; een lekker achterste
body – een lekker lijf; een lekker lichaam; een lekker body
figure – een mooi lichaam
nipples – lekkere tepels
chest – een lekkere borst
hairy chest – een lekker harige borst
legs – lekkere benen

Can I kiss your...? – Kan ik je... zoenen?
Can I suck your...? – Kan ik je... zuigen?
Can I touch your...? – Kan ik je... aanraken?
Can I feel your...? – Kan ik je... voelen?
   cock – lul; pik
   balls – ballen
   bum – billen; kont; achterste
   body – lijf; lichaam; body
   nipples – tepels
   (hairy) chest – (harige) borst
   legs – benen
   toe – teen

That feels good! – Dat voelt lekker!
That's great! – (Dat is) geweldig!
That's wonderful! – (Dat is) fantastisch!
That's really good! – (Dat is) heerlijk/lekker!
Do that again! – (Doe dat) nog eens!
My god, that's wonderful! – Wat geil!
Yes...yes... – Ja...ja...
Come on! – Meer, meer!
Fuck me! – Neuk me!
Suck me! – Pijp me!
Wank me! – Trek me af!
Spank me! – Sla me!
Harder, harder! – Harder, harder!; Sneller, sneller!
Slower slower! – Langzamer, langzamer!
I'm coming...! – Ik kom...!; Ik kom klaar...!
Come all over me! – Kom klaar over mij!
I don't like that! – Dat vind ik niet lekker/prettig!
Stop! – Hou op!; Stop!
That hurts! – Dat doet pijn!
Not so fast/hard! – Niet zo snel/hard!
Don't come in my mouth/arse! – Kom niet in mijn mond/reet!; Haal hem er op tijd uit!
That was wonderful. – Dat was geweldig.
Would you like to clean yourself up? – Wil je je wassen?
Have you got any tissues/ a towel? – Heb je tissues/een handdoek?
Here you are! – Hier!

May I use your shower? – Kan ik een douche nemen?
Shall we have a shower together? – Zullen we een douche nemen?; Zullen we samen douchen?
Can I have a towel (please)? – Kan ik een handdoek hebben (alsjeblieft)?; Heb je handdoek (voor me)?
Good night! – Goede nacht!
Sleep well! – Slaap lekker!
I love you. – Ik hou van je.
Did you sleep well? – Heb je goed geslapen?
I'll have to ask you to leave now – Je moet nu weg.; Ik wil dat je nu weggaat.
Can you go now please? – Ga nu, alsjeblieft.
I have to go now. – Ik moet nu weg.
Would you like some breakfast? – Wil je ontbijten?
Can I write to you? – Kan ik je schrijven?
It's been nice knowing you! – Ik vond het lekker met je!; Leuk je te hebben leren kennen!
Would you like to see me again? – Wil je me weer zien?
Can I see you again? – Kan ik je weer zien/ontmoeten?
Goodbye! – Tot ziens!
See you again! – See you!
Take care! – Pas goed op jezelf!

On the telephone – Aan de telefoon

Hello! – Hallo!
Can I speak with ... (please)? – Kan ik met ... spreken (alstublieft *(formal)* / alsjeblieft *(informal)*)?
Hang on... – Een ogenblikje...
...speaking! – Met...
It's me! – Met mij
It's ... – Met...
I'm phoning you as we arranged. – Ik bel zoals beloofd.
Can we meet ...? – Zullen we elkaar ... ontmoeten?
　this evening – vanavond
　at... o'clock – om ... uur *(see page 78)*
Where? – Waar?
At... – In /Voor/Bij...
Can you spell it? – Kan je dat voor me spellen?

OK, thank you! – OK, bedankt!

See you later! – Tot dan!; Tot straks!

He is not here! – Hij is niet hier; Hij is niet thuis.

Can you phone again... – Kan je... weer bellen?
    later – later
    this afternoon – vanmiddag

I don't understand. – Ik begrijp niet (wat je zegt); Ik begrijp het niet.

Do you speak...? – Spreekt u...?*(formal)*; Spreek je...?*(informal)*

Please speak slowly. – Kunt u langzaam/wat langzamer spreken alstublieft? *(formal)*; Kan je langzaam/wat langzamer spreken alsjeblieft? *(informal)*

Health – Gezondheid

I need to see a doctor. – Ik heb een dokter nodig.

doctor – dokter

surgery [UK]; doctor's office [US] – dokterspraktijk; kliniek

chemist [UK]; pharmacy – drogist; apotheek

I have... – Ik heb...

I have caught... – Ik heb ... opgelopen

I think I have... – Ik denk dat ik ... heb.

Do you have something for...? – Hebt u iets tegen...?
    gonorrhoea – een druiper
    syphilis – syfilis
    crabs – zakratten
    lice – luizen
    herpes – herpes
    scabies – schurft

I hurt here. – Ik heb pijn hier; Het doet hier pijn.

I'm bleeding. – Ik bloed.

I'm itching. – Ik heb jeuk/kriebel.

My throat/penis/anus hurts. – Mijn keel/penis/anus doet pijn.

Services – Dienstverlening

Can you help me? – Kunt u me helpen? *(formal)*; Kun je me helpen? *(informal)*

How much is this/that? – Hoeveel is dit/dat?; Hoeveel kost dit/dat?

Have you got a map of...? – Heb je een kaart van...?

the city – de stad

Can I have the number for Gay Switchboard? – Kan ik het nummer van het gay en lesbische switchboard hebben?

Can I have the number of the AIDS helpline? – Kan ik het nummer van de AIDS hulplijn hebben?

Can you give me the name of a doctor who is experienced in AIDS/HIV-related problems? – Kan je me de naam van een dokter geven die ervaring heeft met AIDS/HIV-verwante problemen?

Can you give me the name of a clinic which is experienced in AIDS/HIV-related problems? – Kan je me de naam van een kliniek geven die ervaring heeft met AIDS/HIV-verwante problemen?

Can you give me the name of a gay-friendly doctor? – Weet jij een dokter die homo-vriendelijk is?

Excuse me! – Pardon!; Sorry!; Neem me niet kwalijk!

Where is/are...? – Waar is/zijn...?
- the sauna – de sauna
- the cruising areas – de baan *(singular noun)*
- the gay bars – de gay bars; de homo bars
- the cottages [UK]; tea rooms [US] – pisbakken; urinoirs *(both meaning public toilets)*
- the gay bookshop – de homo-boekwinkel
- the gay hotels – de gay hotels

Contact ads – Contact advertenties

I am... – Ik ben...

I am looking for a ... guy. – Ik zoek een ... jongen/kerel.

(Adjectives used with masculine nouns such as 'jongen' or 'kerel' must be conjugated. As a general rule, add an -e to the end of the adjective – eg. I am looking for an affectionate guy Ik zoek een hartelijke jongen. Sometimes alterations in spelling are neccesary, in these cases, the conjugated form is given in brackets – eg. I am looking for an active guy Ik zoek een actieve jongen. Adjectives ending in -en are not conjugated with masculine nouns – eg. I am looking for an experienced guy Ik zoek een ervaren jongen).

- **active** – actief (actieve)
- **affectionate** – hartelijk; teder; lief (lieve); aanhankelijk
- **athletic** – atletisch
- **attractive** – attractief (attractieve); aantrekkelijk
- **bisexual** – biseksueel (biseksuele)
- **boyish** – jongensachtig
- **caring** – zorgzaam (zorgzame)
- **Christian** – christelijk
- **chubby** – mollig
- **clean** – schoon (schone); wel verzorgd; net (nette)
- **clean-shaven** – gladgeschoren
- **conservative** – conservatief (conservatieve); behoudend
- **considerate** – attent; zorgzaam (zorgzame)
- **cuddly** – knuffelig; aanhalig; aanhankelijk
- **cute** – leuk; aardig; lekker
- **discreet** – discreet (discrete)
- **dominant** – dominant
- **easy-going** – makkelijk; ongecompliceerd; eenvoudig
- **educated** – ontwikkeld
- **experienced** – ervaren
- **friendly** – vriendelijk; gezellig
- **gentle** – zachtaardig
- **good-looking** – goed uitziend

hairy – behaard
handsome – goed uitziend; mooi; knap (knappe)
honest – eerlijk
horny – geil
I have a good sense of humour – Ik heb een goed gevoel voor humor
independent – zelfstandig; onafhankelijk
inexperienced – onervaren
intelligent – intelligent
interesting – interessant
introverted – introvert
lonely – eenzaam (eenzame)
loyal – trouw; loyaal (loyale)
married – getrouwd; gehuwd
masculine – mannelijk
mature – volwassen
(I am) of medium build – (Ik ben) van gemiddelde lengte; (Ik heb) een normaal postuur
middle aged – van middelbare leeftijd
military – militair
muscular – gespierd
a nature lover – een natuurvriend
non-scene – geen scene type; afkerig van de scene
a non-smoker – een niet-roker
older – ouder
open – open; spontaan (spontane)
open minded – onbevangen; onbevooroordeeld
outgoing – open; spontaan (spontane)
passionate – hartstochtelijk
passive – passief (passieve)
quiet – rustig; stil (stille)
radical – radikaal (radikale)
refined – verfijnd; beschaafd
reliable – betrouwbaar (betrouwbare)
reserved – gereserveerd; terughoudend
romantic – romantisch
sensitive – gevoelig
serious – serieus (serieuze); ernstig
shy – verlegen
sincere – oprecht
slim – slank; mager
a smoker – een roker
smooth – onbehaard
special – speciaal (speciale); bijzonder
spontaneous – spontaan (spontane)
sporty – sportief (sportieve)
straight acting – onopvallend; niet nichterig; niet verwijfd; niet opvallend; niet opzichtig
straight forward – eerlijk; open; oprecht
a student – (een) student
submissive – onderdanig
tall – groot (grote)
transsexual – transseksueel (transseksuele)
(I am) a university graduate – (Ik heb) een universitaire opleiding; (Ik ben) academicus
a virgin – onervaren
warm – warm; hartelijk
well-endowed; well-hung – goed geschapen; groot geschapen; flink geschapen

well-built – goed gebouwd; breed gebouwd; flinkgebouwd
young – jong
younger – jonger
youthful – jeugdig

I am looking for a guy... – Ik zoek een jongen/kerel...
 with a good sense of humour – met een goed gevoel voor humor
 of medium build – van gemiddelde lengte; van normaal postuur
 of the same age – van dezelfde leeftijd

I am looking for a ... guy – Ik zoek een jongen/kerel...
 middle aged – van middelbare leeftijd
 non-scene – die geen scene type is; die afkerig van de scene is

no effeminates – geen nichten; geen verwijfde types

no fats – geen dikkerds

...welcome – ...welkom

for friendship – voor een vriendschap;
 om een vriendschap mee op te bouwen

for a relationship – voor een relatie;
 om een relatie mee op te bouwen

for sex – voor seks

...only – alleen...

I have... – Ik heb...
 blue eyes – blauwe ogen
 brown eyes – bruine ogen
 green eyes – groene ogen
 grey eyes – grijze ogen
 blonde hair – blond haar
 brown hair – bruin haar
 black hair – zwart haar
 red hair – rood haar
 grey hair – grijs haar
 dark hair – donker haar
 short hair – kort haar
 long hair – lang haar

I have a beard. – Ik heb een baard.

I have a moustache. – Ik heb een snor.

I'm bald. – Ik ben kaal.

Expressions – Uitdrukkingen

My God! – Mijn god!

Fantastic! – Fantastisch!

I'm sorry. – Sorry; Het spijt me.

Excuse me! – Sorry!; Neem me niet kwalijk!

Get fucked! – Flikker op!

Fuck off! – Fuck off!
Shit! – Shit!; Verdomme!
Darling! – Lieverd!
My dear! – M'n beste!
Honey! – Schat!
Oh dear! – O jee!
How wonderful! – O, geweldig!
How awful! – Bah!; Vreselijk!; Afschuwelijk!; Wat vies/smerig!
He's a friend of Dorothy. – Hij is ook zo.
As camp as knickers. – Een nicht als een kathedraal.
Wow! – Ooooh!; Goh!; Kijk daar eens!

Other useful vocabulary – Andere handige woorden

Yes. – Ja.
No. – Nee.
I am... – Ik ben...
he is... – hij is...
you are... – mij bent... *(informal)*; U bent... *(formal)*
my friend is... – mijn vriend is...
my friends are... – mijn vrienden zijn...
my boyfriend is... – mijn vriend is...
adult – volwassen
AIDS – AIDS
bent [UK]; homo [US] – van de verkeerde kant
bisexual – biseksueel
a bitch – een (stomme) kut; een kat; een teef
to bitch – katten
bitchy – kattig; hatelijk
body-building – body-building
butch – macho; stoer; tof; butch
camp – nichterig; verwijfd
to chat someone up – iemand opvrijen
to be 'in the closet' – een kastnicht zijn
come; spunk – geil; sperma
to come – (klaar) komen

to 'come out' – (bezig zijn met zijn) 'coming out'
a cow – een (stomme) koe
to cruise – de baan opgaan; iemand oppikken; cruisen
drag – travestie
drag shows – travestieshows
a dyke [UK]; a lesbo [US] – een pot
a butch dyke – een butch pot; een motorpot
erect – erect; stijf
an erection; a hard-on – een erectie; een stijve
a fag hag – een nichtenmoeder
female – vrouwelijk
french-kissing – tongzoenen
a fuck – een neukpartij; neuken; een potje neuken
gay – gay; homo
the gay scene – de gay scene
a girl – een meisje; een meid; een vrouw
a guy – een jongen; een vent; een kerel; een gozer; een knul; een man
the leather scene – de leer scene
a lesbian – a lesbienne (noun); lesbisch (adj.)
male – mannelijk
men only – alleen mannen
the nightclub – de nachtclub
the nudist beach – het naaktstrand
to pick someone up – iemand oppikken
to be pissed off with someone – kwaad zijn op iemand; kotsmisselijk worden van iemand; (I'm pissed off with you) Ik word kotsmisselijk van je; Ik ben je zat.
a poof; a faggot [US] – een flikker; een homo; een poot
a queen – een nicht
queer – homo (adj.); een mietje (noun)
queer-bashing – potenrammen
a rent-boy – een rent boy; een jongensprostitué
SM (sadomasochism) – S & M; sadomasochisme
skinheads – skinheads
a slut – een slons; een del; een slet; een teef
straight – hetero
a tart – een slet; een snol; een del

a transvestite – een travestiet
a wank – aftrekken; een potje aftrekken
women only – alleen vrouwen
one – één
two – twee
three – drie
four – vier
five – vijf
six – zes
seven – zeven
eight – acht
nine – negen
ten – tien
eleven – elf
twelve – twaalf
thirteen – dertien
fourteen – veertien
fifteen – vijftien
sixteen – zestien
seventeen – zeventien
eighteen – achttien
nineteen – negentien
twenty – twintig
twenty one – eenentwintig
twenty two – tweeentwintig
thirty – dertig
forty – veertig
fifty – vijftig
sixty – zestig
seventy – zeventig
eighty – tachtig
ninety – negentig
one hundred – honderd
one thousand – duizend

Talking safer sex!

In the leather bar – In de leer bar

Hello!
Hallo!

Hi!
Hoi!

That's a neat tatoo.
Dat is een aardige tatouage.

Thanks - have you got any?
Dank je - heb jij ook tatouages?

Yeh, on my arse.
Ja, op m'n achterste.

I'd like to see it sometime.
Die zou ik wel eens willen zien.

That can be arranged!
Dat kan!

Do you live far away?
Woon je ver weg?

Just around the corner. Do you want to come back?
Nee, vlakbij. Wil je mee?

Sure!
OK!

  (**On the way home...**
  Op weg naar huis...)

So, what are you into?
Zo, waar hou je van?

Oh you know, sucking, fucking, bondage - most things if it's safe.
Ach, pijpen, neuken, bondage - eigenlijk alles, zo lang het veilig is.

Do you have condoms and lube?
Heb je condooms en glijmiddel?

Plenty - and all strong ones!
Volop - en de sterke!

I don't like sucking cock with condoms.
Ik hou niet van pijpen met condooms.

Neither do I, but I use them all the time for fucking.
Ik ook niet, maar ik gebruik ze altijd om te neuken.

Good.
Goed.

(At home..
Thuis...)

So, you said that you are into bondage.
Zo, je zei dat je van bondage houdt.

Yeah, but not usually on the first date.
Ja, maar niet altijd bij de eerste keer.

Fair enough, let's hope there will be a second!
OK, ik hoop dat er een tweede is!

Oh, I think there will be... now where are those condoms?
Dat denk ik wel... nu, waar zijn die condooms?

Portuguese (with Brazilian Portuguese)

NOTE: [PT] = used in Portugal; [BR] = used in Brazil – 'Formal' language forms are quite common in Brazil amongst friends and when meeting people, whereas in Portugal, the 'informal' forms are used in these contexts.

The Bar/Club – O Bar

I would like... please – Queria ... (por favor); Eu gostaria ... (por favor).
  a half-pint [UK] – uma cerveja pequena; uma imperial [PT]; um chope [BR]
  a pint [UK] – uma cerveja grande
  a beer – uma cerveja
  a light beer – uma cerveja ligeira/light
  a heavy beer [UK] – uma cerveja forte
  a shandy [UK] – uma cerveja com limonada
  a glass of red wine – um copo de vinho tinto
  a glass of white wine – um copo de vinho branco
  a gin and tonic – um gin com tonica; um gin e tonica
  a vodka – uma vodca
  a vodka and coke – uma vodca com coca cola
  a vodka and orange – uma vodca com sumo [PT]/suco [BR] de laranja
  a whisky; a scotch [US] – um uísque; um whisky
  a rum – um rum
  a cider – uma sidra
  a coke – uma coca cola; uma coca
  a lemonade – uma limonada; uma gasosa
  an orange juice – um sumo [PT]/suco [BR] de laranja
  an apple juice – um sumo [PT]/suco [BR] de maçã
  a mineral water – uma água mineral
  a coffee – um café
  white coffee – um café com leite
  a tea – um chá
  hot/cold milk – leite quente/frio
  a hot chocolate – um chocolate quente

with/without – com.../ sem...
  sugar – açúcar
  milk – leite
  ice – gelo
  water – água
  soda – soda
  tonic – tónica
  blackcurrant – groselha negra
  lemon juice – sumo [PT]/suco [BR] de limão

How much is that? – Quanto custa?

Is this seat free? – Este lugar está vago/vazio?
  Yes (it's free). – Sim (está vago/vazio).
  No (it's taken). – Não (está ocupado).

Where are the toilets? – Onde é a casa de banho [PT]/o banheiro [BR]?
  at the back – atrás
  on the right – à direita; ao lado direito
  on the left – à esquerda; ao lado esquerdo
  downstairs – lá em baixo; abaixo
  upstairs – lá em cima; acima

Do you sell anything to eat? – O que é que tem para comer/petiscar?; Tem petiscos?; Tem algo para petiscar [PT]/beliscar [BR]?

something hot/cold – qualquer coisa fria/quente

Have you got a menu? – Tem a ementa? [PT]; Tem a cardápoi? [BR]

Do you sell...? – Vende...?
  matches – fósforos
  cigarettes – cigarros
  poppers – poppers
  condoms; rubbers [US] – preservativos [PT]; camisinhas [BR]
  lubricant – lubrificante

What time does this place close? – A que horas fecha/termina?

What time does this place open? – A que horas abre/começa?

At...o'clock – Às... horas; À ... hora *(with one o'clock)*
  one – uma
  two – duas
  three – três
  four – quatro
  five – cinco
  six – seis
  seven – sete
  eight – oito
  nine – nove
  ten – dez
  eleven – onze
  twelve – doze; à meianoite *(midnight)*; ao meio-dia *(noon)*
  half past one – uma e meia

Cruising – Engatar [PT]; Paquerar [BR]

Hi! – Atão! [PT]; Olá! [PT]; Oi! [BR]

Hello! – Atão! [PT]; Oi! [BR]

Good evening. – Boa noite.

How are you? – Como vais?; Como estás?
  good – bem
  OK – OK; mais ou menos

Do you speak...? – Falas...?
  English – Inglês
  French – Francês
  German – Alemão
  Italian – Italiano
  Spanish – Espanhol
  Dutch – Holandês

Portuguese – Português

Yes (I speak ...). – Sim (eu falo...).
  a bit – um pouco
No (I don't speak...). – Não (eu não falo...).
I'm sorry, I don't speak... – Desculpa, eu não falo...
I don't understand. – Não percebo; Não entendo. [BR]
Can you repeat that (please)? – Podes repetir (se faz favor)? *(informal)*; Podia repetir (se faz favor)? ([BR] *formal)*
Can you speak more slowly please? – Podes falar mais devagar se faz favor? *(informal)*; Podia falar mais devagar se faz favor? ([BR] *formal)*
Have you got a light? – Tens lume/isqueiro/fósforos?
Have you got the time? – Tens horas?; Que horas são?
Thank you! – Obrigado!
Are you on your own? – Estás só/sozinho?
I'm with my boyfriend. – Estou com o meu amigo.
I'm with my friend/friends. – Estou com o meu amigo. *(male friend)*; Estou com a minha amiga. *(female friend)* /Estou com os meus amigos. *(male friends)*; Estou com as minhas amigas. *(female friends)*
What's your name?
  – Como te chamas?;
  Como é o teu nome?
My name is... – Chamo-me... [PT];
  Me chamo... [BR];
  (O) meu nome é...
Where do you come from?
  – De onde és?
I come... – Eu sou...
  from England – da Inglaterra
  from Scotland – da Escócia
  from Wales – do País de Gales
  from Britain – da Grã-Bretanha
  from Ireland – da Irlanda
  from France – da França
  from Germany – da Alemanha
  from Spain – da Espanha
  from Portugal – de Portugal
  from Italy – da Itália
  from Switzerland – da Suiça
  from Belgium – da Bélgica
  from Austria – da Áustria
  from Holland – da Holanda
  from the United States – dos Estados Unidos
  from Canada – do Canadá
  from Brazil – do Brasil

from Japan – do Japão
from Australia – da Austrália
from New Zealand – da Nova Zelândia

Do you come here often? – Vens muitas vezes aqui?

Would you like ...? – Queres...?
a drink – beber alguma coisa; uma bebida
a cigarette – um cigarro

(No, thankyou) I don't smoke. – (Não obrigado,) não fumo.

Are you on holiday [UK]/vacation [US]? – Estás de férias?
Yes (I'm on holiday [UK]/vacation [US]). – Sim (estou de férias).
(No) I work here. – (Não) trabalho aqui.
I study here. – Estudo aqui.

Where do you live? – Onde moras?; Onde vives?

Where are you staying? – Onde estás?

I live... – Moro...; Vivo...

I'm staying... – Estou...
with friends – com amigos
in a hotel – num hotel
in a flat [UK]/apartment [US] – num apartamento
in a house – numa casa

Would you like to go ...? – Queres ir...?
to a cafe a um café
to a restaurant – a um restaurante
to another bar – a outro bar
to a disco – a uma discoteca
to a sauna – a uma sauna
to the beach – à praia
to the pool – à piscina
for a walk – dar uma volta

Would you like to... with me? – Queres... comigo?
dance – dançar
have a drink – beber
have something to eat – ir comer

Can I buy you a drink? – Posso te oferecer uma bebida?

What would you like (to drink)? – O que é que queres (beber)?

It's ... here tonight, (isn't it?) – Está ... hoje, (não está?) [PT];
    Tá ... hoje, (num tá?) [BR]
packed – lotado; super lotado
busy – cheio; animado
dead – morto
boring – aborrecido [PT]; chato

I like your... – Eu gosto...
jacket – do teu casaco [PT]/paletó [BR]
shirt – da tua camisa
clothes – da tua roupa
haircut – do teu corte de cabelo

Where did you get it/them from? – Onde è que compraste?
Where did you get your hair done? – Onde è que cortaste o cabelo?
You look very smart/nice tonight! – Estás elegante/geitoso hoje!
How old are you? – Quantos anos tens?
I'm... (years old). – Tenho ... anos.
(see numbers on page 112)
Nice eyes! – Olhos bonitos!
Nice legs! – Boas pernas!
Nice bum! – Rico cú! [PT]; Bunda bonita! [BR]
What a nice smile you have! – Tens um sorriso lindo/bonito!
You're... – Tu és...
  beautiful – belo; lindo; formoso; engraçado
  handsome – bonito; gato [BR]
  hunky – forte; atlético; matulão [PT]; gostoso [BR]
  a hunk – um (rico) matulão [PT]; um gatão [BR]
  gorgeous – lindo; gostoso [BR]; bonitão [BR]
  sweet – meigo; bonitinho
  cute – borrachinho [PT]; borracho [PT]; bonitinho [BR]; gracinha [BR]
  sexy – sexy
  attractive – atraente
You really turn me on. – Tu dás-me tesão.
You really make me hot. – Tu és quente [PT]; Tu és fogoso. [BR]
I'm crazy about you. – Eu sou louco por ti.
You're not my type. – Tu não és o meu tipo.
I'm not interested. – Não estou interessado; Não estou afim. [BR]
Get lost! – Deixa-me em paz!; Desaparece!; Se manda! [BR]
Piss off! – Vai à merda!
What type of guys do you like? – Qual é o teu tipo?
What are you into? – Do que é que gostas?
I'm into... – Eu gosto...
I'm not into...; I don't like... – Eu não gosto...
  older men – de homens maduros; dos quarentões [PT]; de coroa [BR]
  younger men – de jovens
  blonde guys – de loiros [PT]; de louros [BR]
  guys with brown hair – de tips [PT]/caras[BR] com cabelo castanho
  guys with dark hair – de tipos [PT]/caras [BR] com cabelo preto
  red heads – de ruivos
  guys with short hair – de tipos [PT]/caras [BR] com cabelo curto
  guys with long hair – de tipos [PT]/caras [BR] com cabelo comprido [PT]/longo[BR]
  hunky guys; well-built guys – de tipos fortes [PT]; de caras fortes/gostosos [BR]
  thin guys – de rapazes magros
  chubby guys – de rapazes gorduchos
  tall guys – de rapazes altos
  short guys – de baixos

- **guys with dark eyes** – de tipos [PT]/caras[BR] com olhos castanhos
- **guys with blue eyes** – de tipos [PT]/caras[BR] com olhos azúis
- **denim** – de brim; de jeans; de vaqueiras; de zuarte [PT]
- **leather** – de couro
- **rubber** – de roupa de borracha
- **dildos** – de vibradores; de consolos[BR]
- **water sports** – que me mijem encima
- **fisting** – de enfiar a mão no cú
- **threesomes** – de menage à trois
- **cross-dressing** – de travestir-me [PT]; de me travestir [BR]
- **piercing** – de brinco
- **tattoos** – de tatuagens
- **boots** – de botas
- **uniforms** – de uniformes
- **brown; scat** – que me caguem encima
- **bondage** – de servir de escravo

Is there somewhere quieter/more private we can go? – Há algum sitio sossegado/mais privado aonde podemos ir?

Do you want to come to my place? – Queres vir comigo?

Yes. – Sim.

I'm sorry, I can't. – Não, não posso.

Can we meet again? – Quando nos vemos?

When? – Quando?

Would you like to meet me…? – Queres ver-me de novo…? [PT]; Queres me ver de novo…? [BR]
- **this evening** – hoje à noite
- **tomorrow** – amanhã
- **tomorrow morning** – amanhã de manhã
- **tomorrow afternoon** – amanhã à tarde [PT]; amanhã de tarde [BR]
- **tomorrow night** – amanhã à noite [PT]; amanhã de noite [BR]
- **on Monday** – na segunda-feira
- **on Tuesday** – na terça-feira
- **on Wednesday** – na quarta-feira
- **on Thursday** – na quinta-feira
- **on Friday** – na sexta-feira
- **on Saturday** – no sábado
- **on Sunday** – no domingo

At what time? – Que horas?; A que horas?

At … o'clock – À…*(with one o'clock)*; Às… *(otherwise) (see page 97)*

Where? – onde?
- **here** – aqui
- **at my hotel** – no meu hotel
- **at my flat [UK]/apartment [US]** – no meu apartamento
- **at my house** – na minha casa
- **at my friend's place** – na casa de meu amigo
- **at your place** – na tua casa

Can I have your phone number? – Dá-me o teu (número do) telefone! [PT]; Me dê seu (número do) telefone! [BR]

Can I have your address? – Dá-me a tua morada! [PT]; Me dê seu endereço! [BR]

Bye. – Tchau; Adeus [PT].
Goodbye. – Até logo; Adeus [PT].
See you again! – Até à vista [PT]; Até breve [PT]; A gente vê-se [PT]; A gente se vê [BR]

At his place/your place – A sua casa/tua casa

Would you like some...? – Queres...?
  coffee – um café
  tea – um chá
  wine – um vinho
  orange juice – um sumo [PT]/suco [BR] de laranja?

Would you like something to eat? – Queres comer alguma coisa?

Are you hungry/thirsty? – Tens fome/sede?

Are you cold/too hot? – Tens frio/muito calor?

Do you want to watch TV/a video? – Queres ver TV/um video? [PT]; Queres assistir TV/um video? [BR]

Would you like to listen to some music? – Queres ouvir música?

What kind of music do you like? – Que tipo de música gostas?
  classical – clássica
  opera – ópera
  jazz – jazz
  rock – rock
  pop – pop
  folk – folk
  traditional – tradicional

Can I kiss you? – Posso dar-te um beijo?

Would you like...? – Gostarias de...?
  a massage – uma massagem
  a blow job – um broche [PT]; uma mamada [PT]; uma chupeta [BR]

What do you like doing? – O que gostas de fazer?

I like... – Eu gosto...

I don't like... – Eu não gosto...

Do you like...? – Gostas...?
  kissing – de beijar
  cuddling – de abraçar
  fucking – de foder; de trepar; de enrabar
  being fucked – de ser fodido; de ser trepado; de ser enrabado
  sucking – de mamar [PT]; de chupar [BR]
  being sucked – de ser mamado [PT]; de ser chupado [BR]
  wanking; jerking off [US] – de bater uma punheta; de masturbar-me [PT]; de me masturbar [BR] (*Do you like...? Gostas de te masturbar ?*)
  mutual masturbation – de masturbação mútua; de punheta mútua
  licking – de lamber
  stroking – de acariciar
  rubbing – de esfregar

spanking – de açoitar; de dar açoites *(softer)*; de dar palmadas *(harder)*
being spanked – de levar açoites *(softer)*; de levar palmadas *(harder)*
cross-dressing – de travestir-me [PT]; de me travestir [BR]; *(Do you like cross-dressing? Gostas de te travestir?)*
shaving – de barbear os pelos do corpo; de raspar os pelos
fisting – de enfiar a mão no cú
rimming – de lamber cú; de lingua no cú

Are you..?/I am ... – Tu és...?/ Eu sou...
experienced – experiente
inexperienced – inexperiente

I like to be... – Eu prefiro ser...
active – activo
passive – passivo

Shall we go to the bedroom/bathroom? – Vamos para o quarto/quarto de banho?

Have you got any...? – Tens alguns...?
condoms; rubbers [US] – preservativos [PT]; camisinhas [BR]
toys – jogos sexuáis
lubricant – lubrificante
poppers – poppers

Are you into safer sex? – Fazes sexo com segurança?; Fazes sexo seguro?

I'm only into safer sex. – Eu só faço sexo com cuidado; Eu só faço sexo seguro.

I'm HIV-positive. – Eu sou seropositivo.

Are you HIV-positive? – Tu és seropositivo?

Would you like a shower (with me)? – Queres tomar um duche [PT]/uma ducha [BR] (comigo)?; Queres tomar um banho (comigo)?

Take off...! – Tira...!

Can I take off...? – Posso tirar...?
your clothes – a tua roupa
your shirt – a tua camisa
your trousers; your pants [US] – as tuas calças
your socks – as tuas meias; as tuas peúgas [PT]
your briefs; your underpants; your shorts [US] – as tuas cuecas; os teus calções; o teu short [BR]

Lie down! – Deita-te! [PT]; Deita! [BR]

Bend over! – Inclina-te [PT]; Fica de quatro! [BR]

Sit down! – Senta-te! [PT]; Senta! [BR]

You're really nice. – Eu gosto de ti; Tu és ótimo. [BR]

I like... – Eu gosto...
your cock – do teu pau; do teu caralho; do teu penis; do teu cacete; da tua picha [PT]; da tua tranca [PT]; da tua porra [BR]; do teu pinto [BR]
your balls – dos teus colhões; dos teus ovos [BR]
your bum – do teu traseiro [PT]; do teu cú [PT]; da tua bunda [BR]
your body – do teu corpo

    your figure – do teu corpo
    your nipples – dos teus mamilos; das tuas tetas [PT]
    your (hairy) chest – do teu peito (cabeludo/peludo)
    your legs – das tuas pernas

Can I kiss...? – Posso beijar...?

Can I suck...? – Posso mamar [PT]/chupar [BR]...?

Can I touch...? – Posso tocar ...?

Can I feel...? – Posso sentir...?
    your cock – o teu pau; o teu caralho; o teu penis; o teu cacete; a tua picha [PT]; a tua tranca [PT]; a tua porra [BR]; o teu pinto [BR]
    your balls – os teus colhões; os teus ovos [BR]
    your bum – o teu traseiro [PT]; o teu cú [PT]; a tua bunda [BR]
    your body – o teu corpo
    your figure – o teu corpo
    your nipples – os teus mamilos; as tuas tetas [PT]
    your (hairy) chest – o teu peito (cabeludo/peludo)
    your legs – as tuas pernas
    your toe – o dedo grande do teu pé

That feels good! – Ai que bom!

That's great! – Fantástico!; Óptimo [PT]; Ótimo [BR]

That's wonderful! – Isso é maravilhoso!

That's really good! – Isso é muito bom!

Do that again! – Faz outra vez!

My god, that's wonderful! – Do caralho! [PT]; Tu és muito bom!

Yes...yes... – Sim...sim...

Come on! – Anda!; Vamos!; Vêm-te! [PT]; Venha! [BR]

Fuck me! – Fode-me!; Trepa-me!; Enraba-me!

Suck me! – Mama-me! [PT]; Chupa-me! [BR]

Wank me! – Bate-me uma punheta!

Spank me! – Açoita-me !

Harder, harder! – Mais força!

Slower, slower! – Devagar, devagar!

I'm coming...! – Estou-me a vir...! [PT]; Estou gozando...! [BR]

Come all over me! – Vem-te encima de mim!

I don't like that! – Eu não gosto disso!

Stop! – Pare!

That hurts! – Isso faz-me doer!

Not so fast/hard! – Mais devagar!/Com menos força!

Don't come in my mouth/arse! – Não te venhas na minha boca/no meu cú! [PT]; Não goze na minha boca/no meu cú! [BR]

That was wonderful. – Foi muito bom.
Would you like to clean yourself up? – Queres te limpar?
Have you got any tissues/ a towel? – Tens lenço de papel/uma toalha?
Here you are! – Está aqui!
May I use your shower? – Posso usar o teu duche [PT]/tua ducha [BR]?
Shall we have a shower together? – Vamos tomar um duche [PT]/uma ducha [BR] juntos?; Vamos tomar banho juntos?
Can I have a towel (please)? – Dá-me uma toalha! [PT]; Me dê uma toalha! [BR]
Good night! – Boa noite!
Sleep well! – Dorme bem!
I love you. – Eu amo-te [PT]; Eu te amo. [BR]
Did you sleep well? – Dormiste bem?
I'll have to ask you to leave now. – Tenho muita pena mas tens de te ir embora imediatamente.
Can you go now please? – Podes ir-te embora já se faz favor?
I have to go now. – Eu tenho de me ir embora já!
Would you like some breakfast? – Queres café?
Can I write to you? – Posso te escrever?
It's been nice knowing you! – Foi bom conhecer-te! [PT]; Foi bom te conhecer! [BR]
Would you like to see me again? – Queres encontrar-te comigo outra vez?
Can I see you again? – Podemos encontrar-mo-nos outra vez?
Goodbye! – Até logo!; Adeus! [PT]
See you again! – Até breve! [PT]; A gente vê-se! [PT]; A gente se vê! [BR]
Take care. – Até à próxima!

On the telephone – Ao telefone

Hello! – Está! [PT]; Alô! [BR]
Can I speak with ... (please)? – Posso falar com...?
Hang on... – Um momento...
...speaking! – Daqui fala o...!
It's me! – Sou eu aqui!
It's ... – Sou...
I'm phoning you as we arranged. – Estou a telefonar como o combinado [PT]; Estou telefonando como o combinado. [BR]
Can we meet ...? – Podemo-nos encontrar...?
   this evening – hoje à noite

at... o'clock – às... horas; à... hora *(with one o'clock) (see page 97)*

Where? – Onde?

At... – Em...; Na...; No...

Can you spell it? – Pode soletrar se faz favor? ([BR] *or formal in Portugal*); Podes soletrar? *(informal)*

OK, thank you! – OK obrigado!

See you later! – Vemo-nos! [PT]; Nos vemos! [BR]

He is not here! – Ele não está!

Can you phone again... – Pode chamar/telefonar de novo...
   later – mais tarde; depois
   this afternoon – esta tarde; pela tarde

I don't understand. – Não percebo; Não entendo. [BR]

Do you speak...? – Você fala...? ([BR] *or formal in Portugal*); Falas...?*(informal)*

Please speak slowly. – Fala devagar, por favor. ([BR] *or formal in Portugal*); Fale devagar, por favor.*(informal)*

Health – Saúde

I need to see a doctor. – Preciso de um médico.

doctor – médico

surgery [UK]; doctor's office [US] – consultório

chemist [UK]; pharmacy – farmácia

I have... – Eu tenho...

I have caught... – Eu contraí...

I think I have... – Parece-me que tenho... [PT]; Me parece que tenho... [BR]

Do you have something for...? – Tem algo contra ...?
   gonorrhoea – gonorreia
   syphilis – sífilis
   crabs – chatos
   lice – piolhos
   herpes – herpes
   scabies – sarna

I hurt here. – Dói-me aqui.

I'm bleeding. – Estou perdendo sangue.

I'm itching. – Tenho comichão.

My throat/penis/anus hurts. – Dói-me a garganta/o pénis/o anus.

Services – Serviço

Can you help me? – Podia ajudar-me?([BR] *or formal in Portugal*); Podes ajudar-me? *(informal)*

How much is this/that? – Quanto é (que custa)?; Quanto custa isso?
Have you got a map of...? – Você tem um mapa da/do/de... ?
the city – da cidade
Can I have the number for Gay Switchboard? – Poderia me dar o (número do) telefone do informativo gay?
Can I have the number of the AIDS helpline? – Poderia me dar o número do telefone da ajuda SIDA?[PT]; Poderia me dar o (número do) telefone do disque AIDS? [BR]
Can you give me the name of a doctor who is experienced in AIDS/HIV-related problems? – Poderia me dar o nome de um médico especializado nos problemas relacionados com o SIDA [PT]/AIDS [BR] /a seropositividade?
Can you give me the name of a clinic which is experienced in AIDS/HIV-related problems? – Poderia me dar o nome de uma clinica especializada nos problemas relacionados com o SIDA [PT]/AIDS [BR] /a seropositividade?
Can you give me the name of a gay-friendly doctor? – Pode-me dar o nome de um médico que simpatize com gays?
Excuse me! – Desculpe!
Where is/are...? – Onde é/são...?
    the sauna – a sauna
    the cruising areas – os pontos de encontro; os pontos de paquera [BR]
    the gay bars – os bares gay
    the cottages [UK]; tea rooms [US] – as retretes [PT]; as capelinhas [PT]; os banheiros de pegação [BR]
    the gay bookshop – a livraria gay
    the gay hotels – os hotéis gays

Contact ads – Contactos

I am... – Eu sou...
I am looking for a ... guy – Procuro um tipo [PT]/cara [BR]...
    active – activo
    affectionate – afectuoso; carinhoso
    athletic – atlético
    attractive – atraente
    bisexual – bissexual
    boyish – muito jóven; pueril
    caring – bondoso
    Christian – cristão
    chubby – roliço; gorducho
    clean – limpo
    clean-shaven – de cara/face barbeada
    conservative – conservador
    considerate – atencioso
    cuddly – acariciável [PT]; fofo [BR]

cute – bonitinho; gracinha; borrachinho [PT]; borracho [PT]
discreet – discreto
dominant – dominador
easy-going – pacato; fácil
educated – educado
experienced – experiente; com experiência
friendly – simpático; amigável
gentle – amável; doce; leve; suave
good-looking – bonito; bonitão; geitoso
hairy – peludo; cabeludo
handsome – bonito; gato [BR]
honest – honesto
horny – com tesão; entesoado [PT]
with a good sense of humour – com bom senso de humor (*I have a good sense of humour* Eu tenho um bom senso de humor)
independent – independente
inexperienced – inexperiente; sem experiência
intelligent – inteligente
interesting – interessante
introverted – introvertido
lonely – só
loyal – leal
married – casado
masculine – másculo; viril; machão
mature – maduro
of medium build – de tamanho medio
middle aged – de meia-idade
military – militar
muscular – musculoso
a nature lover – amante da natureza
non-scene – fora de ambiente; fora de cena
(a) non-smoker – (um) não-fumador [PT]; (um) não-fumante [BR]
older – mais velho
open aberto
open minded – aberto; imparcial
outgoing – extrovertido; sociável
passionate – apaixonado
passive – passivo
quiet – quieto; tranquilo
radical – radical
refined – refinado; culto
reliable – confiável; sério; de confiança
reserved – reservado
romantic – romântico
of the same age – da mesma idade
sensitive – sensível
serious – sério
shy – tímido
sincere – sincero; franco
slim – magro; esbelto; delgado
(a) smoker – (um) fumador [PT]; (um) fumante [BR]
smooth – macio
special – especial
spontaneous – espontâneo

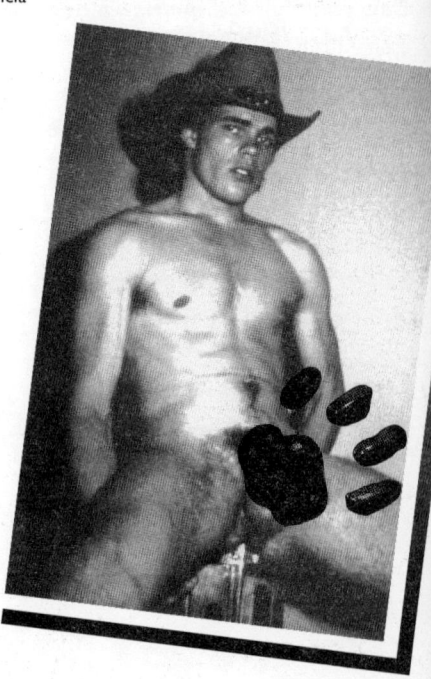

sporty – desportivo [PT]; esportivo [BR]
straight acting – não efeminado
straight forward – directo [PT]; direte [BR]
(a) student – (um) estudante; (um) universitário
submissive – submisso
tall – alto
transexual – transsexual
(a) university graduate – graduado; licenciado; laureado [PT]
(a) virgin – virgem
warm – afectuoso
well-endowed; well-hung – bem dotado; com caralhão; com uma boa moca [PT] (*I am...* Tenho um caralhão/uma boa moca [PT])
well-built – robusto; atlético
young – jovem
younger – mais jovem
youthful – juvenil

no effeminates – não efeminados

no fats – não gorduchos

...welcome – ...bem-vindo (*-s if plural*)

for friendship – para amizade

for a relationship – para relação

for sex – para sexo

...only – somente...

I have... – Eu tenho...
  blue eyes – olhos azúis
  brown eyes – olhos castanhos
  green eyes – olhos verdes
  grey eyes – olhos cinzentos
  blonde hair – cabelo loiro
  brown hair – cabelo castanho
  black hair – cabelo preto
  red hair – cabelo ruivo
  grey hair – cabelo grisalho/branco
  dark hair – cabelo preto
  short hair – cabelo curto
  long hair – cabelo longo

I have a beard. – Tenho barba.

I have a moustache. – Tenho um bigode/uma grande bigodaça [PT] (*big bushy moustache*).

I'm bald. – Sou careca.

Expressions – Expressões

My God! – Meu Deus!
Fantastic! – Fantástico!
I'm sorry. – Desculpa!

Excuse me! – Com licença!
Get fucked! – Vai te foder!
Fuck off! – Vai levar no cú! [PT]; Vai tomar no cú! [BR]
Shit! – Merda!; Que saco! [BR]
Darling! – Querido!
My dear! – Meu querido!
Honey! – Querido!; Mel!
Oh dear! – Ai!
How wonderful! – Que maravilhoso!
How awful! – Horrível!
He's a friend of Dorothy. – É uma irmã [PT]; É (um) entendido [PT]
As camp as knickers. – É muito amaricado/maricas [PT]; Desmunheca como uma louca [BR].
Wow! – Caramba!

Other useful vocabulary – Outro vocabulario útil

Yes. – Sim.
No. – Não.
I am... – eu sou...
he is... – ele é...
you are... – tu és... *(informal)*; você é... *([BR]formal)*
my friend is... – o meu amigo é... *(male friend)*/a minha amiga é... *(female friend)*
my friends are... – os meus amigos são... *(male friends)*/as minhas amigas são... *(female friends)* *(adj. + -s)*
my boyfriend is... – o meu amigo é...
adult – adulto
AIDS – SIDA [PT]; AIDS [BR]
bent [UK]; homo [US] – invertido
bisexual – bissexual
a bitch – uma cadela; uma vagabunda; uma meretriz; uma puta; uma rameira
to bitch – criticar
bitchy – criticas
body-building – musculação
butch – machão *(fem. machona)*
camp – afectado; efeminado; afetado [BR]
to chat someone up – engatar [PT]; paquerar [BR]

to be 'in the closet' – não declarado
come; spunk – gozo; esperma
to come – vir-se [PT]; gozar [BR]
to 'come out' – declarar-se [PT]; assumir [BR]
a cow – uma vaca
to cruise – engatar [PT]; andar ao engate [PT]; paquerar [BR]
drag – em travesti
drag shows – espectáculos de travesti [PT]; shows de travesti [BR]
a dyke [UK]; a lesbo [US] – uma machona; uma sapatão [BR]
a butch dyke – uma mulher macho
erect – erecto; erguido; entesar
an erection; a hard-on – um erecção; um entesoado [PT]
a fag hag – uma mulher que acompanha gays
female – feminino
french-kissing – beijo de lingua *(noun)*; fazer linguado *(verb)*
a fuck – uma foda
gay – gay; bicha; entendido
the gay scene – o ambiente gay
a girl – uma jovem; uma moça; uma rapariga [PT]; uma mina [BR]
a guy – um tipo [PT]; um gajo [PT]; uma pessoa [PT]; um sujeito; um cara [BR]; um moço; um rapaz
the leather scene – o ambiente de (roupa) couro
a lesbian – uma lésbica *(noun)*; lésbico *(adj.)*
male – masculino
men only – só para homens
the nightclub – o nightclub
the nudist beach – a praia nudista
to pick someone up – buscar alguém; engatar [PT]; paquerar [BR]
to be pissed off with someone – estar chateado com alguém
a poof; a faggot [US] – uma bicha; um paneleiro [PT]; um maricas [PT]; um rabão [PT]; um rabicho [PT]
a queen – um maricas [PT]; um larilas [PT]; uma bichona [PT]; uma perua [BR]; uma fada [BR]; uma princesa [BR]
queer – maricas [PT]; bicha
queer-bashing – atacar homosexuais
a rent-boy – um garoto de aluguer; um chulo (de homens); um michê [BR]

SM (sadomasochism) – sadomasoquismo
skinheads – cabeças rapadas; carecas
a slut – uma mulher da vida; uma puta; um coiro; uma vaca
straight – hetero
a tart – uma puta [PT]; uma piranha [BR]
a transvestite – um travesti
a wank – uma punheta
women only – só para mulheres
one – um
two – duas
three – três
four – quatro
five – cinco
six – seis
seven – sete
eight – oito
nine – nove
ten – dez
eleven – onze
twelve – doze
thirteen – treze
fourteen – catorze
fifteen – quinze
sixteen – dezaseis
seventeen – dezasete
eighteen – dezoito
nineteen – dezanove
twenty – vinte
twenty one – vinte e um
twenty two – vinte e dois
thirty – trinta
forty – quarenta
fifty – cinquenta
sixty – sessenta
seventy – setenta

eighty – oitenta
ninety – noventa
one hundred – cem
two hundred – duzentos
three hundred – trezentos
four hundred – quatrocentos
five hundred – quinhentos
six hundrerd – seiscentos
seven hundred – setecentos
eight hundred – oitocentos
nine hundred – novecentos
one thousand – mil

Talking safer sex!
In the bar – No bar

Hi!
Olá!

Hello!
Olá!

Do you know where the toilet is?
Sabes aonde è a retrete?

No, I haven't been here before.
Não, não conheço este sítio.

Oh, I thought you looked worried.
Ah! Parece-me que estavas preocupado.

I haven't been anywhere gay before.
Nunca visitei um lugar gay.

Well, have a good time...I'll see you later.
Bem, diverte-te...Até à próxima.

(Three hours later...
Três horas mais tarde...)

Hello again. Been having a good time?
Olá, tens-te divertido?

Not really.
Na realidade, não!

Why's that?
Então porquê?

I can't get the hang of this.
Não me consigo habituar a isto!

Do you want a drink?
Queres uma bebida?

Yes, a coke please.
Sim, uma coca se faz favor.

(Later still...
Mais tarde...)

...so then my parents chucked me out and I moved here.
...então os meus pais puseram-me na rua e vim para aqui.

Well, that's some story. Do you want to come back to my place for a coffee?
Bem, que grande historia. Queres vir a minha casa tomar um café?

That would be good.
Sim, muito obrigado.

(In the bedroom...
No quarto...)

This is scary.
Não estou habituado a estas coisas.

Why?
Porquê?

Well, you know, AIDS and everything. I don't want to get it.
Bem, sabes SIDA etc, não quero apanhar a SIDA.

Neither do I! But there's no risk with most things you can do.
Nem eu! Não há risco na maior parte do que fazemos.

What do you mean?
Não percebo.

Well, unless you fuck without a condom, you are pretty safe.
Quero dizer, se te foder com preservativo não há perigo.

Are you sure?
Tens a certeza?

Sure I'm sure. What we've just been doing, wanking, kissing, sucking, they are all safe as far as HIV is concerned. Don't worry about it.
Tenho certeza absoluta. O que nós temos estado a fazer, punhetas, beijar, mamar, não houve perigo de contágio no que diz respeito a ficar seropositivo. Não estejas preocupado.

Brilliant!
Óptimo!

Japanese

The Bar/Club – Gei bā de

I would like... please – ... o kudasai!; ...onegaishimasu!
  a half-pint [UK]/a pint [UK] – *(don't exist in Japan, all beer comes in the same sized glasses)*
  a beer – Biiru
  a light beer – Raito biiru
  a heavy beer [UK] – Kuro biiru
  a shandy [UK] – Shandii; Biiru no remonēdo wari
  a glass of red wine – Aka wain
  a glass of white wine – Shiro wain
  a gin and tonic – Jintonikku
  a vodka – Uokka
  a vodka and coke – Uokka no kōra wari
  a vodka and orange – Uokka no orenji wari
  a whisky; a scotch [US] – Uisukii
  a rum – Ramu
  a cider – Saidā
  a coke – Koka kōra
  a lemonade – Remonēdo
  an orange juice – Orenji jūsu
  an apple juice – Appuru jūsu
  a mineral water – Mineraru uōtā
  a coffee – Kōhii
  white coffee – Kafe ōre
  a tea – Kōcha
  hot/cold milk – Hotto/Aisu miruku
  a hot chocolate – Kokoa

with... – ...o irete; ...no...wari *(both: reverse word order to English)*

without... – ...nashi de *(reverse word order to English)*
  sugar – satō
  milk – miruku
  ice – kōri
  water – mizu
  soda – sōda
  tonic – tonikku
  blackcurrant – kashisu
  lemon juice – remon jūsu

How much is that? – Ikura desuka?

Is this seat free? – Koko aitemasuka?
  Yes (it's free). – Hai (aitemasu).
  No (it's taken). – Iie (aitemasen).

Where are the toilets? – Toire wa doko desuka?

at the back – ushiro desu
on the right – migi desu
on the left – hidari desu
downstairs – shita desu
upstairs – ue desu

Do you sell anything to eat? – Nanika taberumono arimasuka?

something hot/cold – atatakaimono/tsumetaimono

Have you got a menu? – Menyū wa arimsuka?

Do you sell...? – ...arimasuka?
   matches – Matchi
   cigarettes – Tabako
   poppers – Rasshu
   condoms – Kondōmu
   lube; lubricant – Zerii

What time does this place close/open? – Nanji ni koko shimarimasuka/akimasuka?

At...o'clock – ...ji.
   one – ichi
   two – ni
   three – san
   four – yo *(used with time expressions, otherwise 'yon')*
   five – go
   six – roku
   seven – shichi
   eight – hachi
   nine – ku *(used with time expressions, otherwise 'kyū')*
   ten – jū
   eleven – jūichi
   twelve – jūni
   half past one – ichi ji han

Cruising – Hatten suru

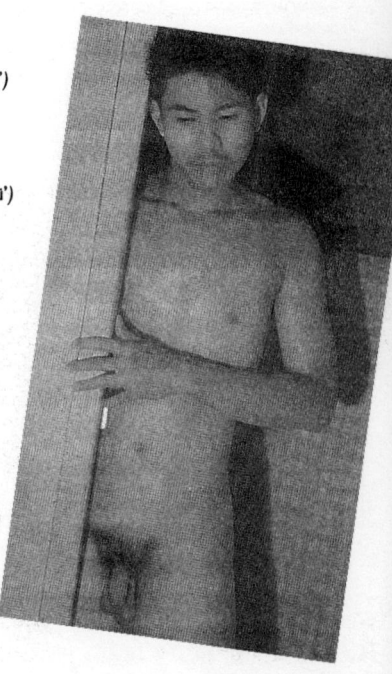

Hi! – Hāi!; Genki?

Hello! – Konnichi wa!

Good evening. – Konban wa.

How are you? – Genki?
   good – un genki *(informal)* ; Hai genki desu *(formal)*
   OK – mā mā

Do you speak...? – ... hanasemasuka?
   English – Eigo
   French – Furansugo
   German – Doitsugo
   Italian – Itariago
   Spanish – Supeingo
   Portuguese – Porutogarugo
   Dutch – Orandago
   Japanese - Nihongo

Yes (I speak ...). – Hai (...hanasemasu).
   a bit – sukoshi
No (I don't speak...). – Iie (...hanasemasen).
I'm sorry, I don't speak ... – Sumimasen, ...hanasemasen.
I don't understand. – Wakaranai *(informal)* ; Wakarimasen. *(formal)*
Can you repeat that (please)? – Mōichido. *(informal)* ; Mōichido onegaishimasu. *(formal)*
Can you speak more slowly please? – Yukkuri onegaishimasu.*(informal)* ; Mōsukoshi yukkuri hanashite kudasai.*(formal)*
Have you got a light? – Raitā/Hi motteru? *(informal)* ; Raitā/Hi arimasuka? *(formal)*
Have you got the time? – Ima nanji?
Thank you! – Arigatō!; Dōmo!
Are you on your own? – Hitori de kiteruno?
I'm with my boyfriend. – Kare/Kareshi to issho.
I'm with my friend/friends. – Tomodachi to issho.
What's your name? – Namae wa?
My name is... – ...(desu)
Where do you come from? – Doko kara kitano?
I come from... – ...kara (desu)
   England – Ingurando
   Scotland – Sukottorando
   Wales – Uēruzu
   Britain – Igirisu
   Ireland – Airurando
   France – Furansu
   Germany – Doitsu
   Spain – Supein
   Portugal – Porutogaru
   Italy – Itaria
   Switzerland – Suisu
   Belgium – Berugii
   Austria – Ōsutoria
   Holland – Oranda
   the United States – Amerika
   Canada – Kanada
   Japan – Nihon
   Australia – Ōsutoraria
   New Zealand – Nyū jiirando

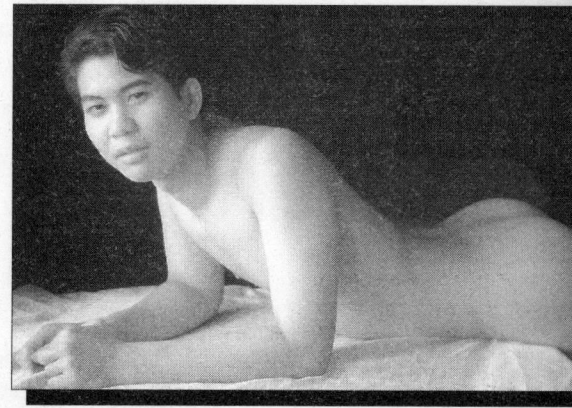

Do you come here often? – Koko ni yoku kuruno?
Would you like ...? – ...hoshii? (informal) ; ...hoshiidesuka ? (formal)
   a drink – Nanika nomumono
   a cigarette – Tabako
(No, thank you) I don't smoke. – (Ii desu) tabako wa suimasen.
Are you on holiday [UK]/vacation [US]? – Ryokō de kiteruno?

Yes (I'm on holiday). – Hai, (sō desu).
(No) I work here. – (Iie,) Koko de hataraitemasu.
I study here. – Koko de benkyō shitemasu; Gakusei desu.

Where do you live? – Doko ni sunde imasuka?
Where are you staying? – Doko ni tomatte imasuka?
I live... – ...sundeimasu
I'm staying... – ...tomatteimasu
   with friends – Tomodachi no tokoro ni *(used with 'I'm staying')*; Tomodachi to *(used with 'I live')*
   in a hotel – Hoteru ni
   in a flat [UK]/apartment [US] – Apāto ni
   in a house – ie ni

Would you like to go ...? – ...ni ikitai? *(informal)*; ...ni ikitaidesuka? *(formal)*
   to a cafe – Kissa ten
   to a restaurant – Resutoran
   to another bar – Betsu no bā
   to a disco – Disuko
   to a sauna – Sauna
   to the beach – Umi
   to the pool – Pūru
   for a walk – Sanpo

Would you like to ... with me? – Watashi/Boku to...tai?
   dance – odori
   have a drink – nomi
   have something to eat – isshoni nanika tabe
   Would you like to have something to eat with me? – Isshoni dokoka e tabeni ikimasenka?

Can I buy you a drink? – Ippai ogorōka? *(informal)*; Ippai ogorimashōka? *(formal)*
What would you like (to drink)? – Nani o nomitai?
It's ... here tonight, (isn't it?) – Konya wa ... ne!
   packed – totemo konderu
   busy – konderu
   dead – zenzen hitoga inai
   boring – tsumaranai

I like your ... – Kimi no ... ii ne!
   jacket – jaketto
   shirt – shatsu
   clothes – fuku
   haircut – hea sutairu

Where did you get it/them from? – Doko de kattano?
Where did you get your hair done? – Doko de kattano?
You look very smart/nice tonight! – Kyō (kimi) sugoku oshare/kakkoii ne!
How old are you? – Ikutsu?; Nansai?
I'm...(years old). – ...sai.
(see numbers on page 132)

Nice eyes! – Kirei na me da ne!

Nice legs! – Kirei na ashi da ne!

Nice bum! – Ii ketsu shiteru ne! *(with friends)*; Ii oshiri da ne!*(with strangers)*

What a nice smile you have! – Egaoga ii ne!

You're... – (Kimi wa) ... (ne!). *(In Japanese, it is enough to use the adjective only to be understood)*
  beautiful – kirei; kakkoii; ii otoko
  handsome – hansamu
  hunky – ii karada; matcho
  a hunk – matcho; ii karada; kakkoii
  gorgeous – kakkoii; ikeru; suteki
  sweet – amai; kawaii
  cute – kawaii
  sexy – sekushii
  attractive – ikeru; miryokuteki

(The following three expressions are not used much in Japanese, and could cause embarrassment!)

You really turn me on. – Kimi wa hontō ni boku o kōfun saseru (yo).

You really make me hot. – Kimi wa hontō ni boku o atsuku saseru (yo).

I'm crazy about you. – Kimi ni mō muchū (dayo).

You're not my type. – Kimi wa boku no taipu janai.

I'm not interested. – Kyōmi nai.

Get lost! – Atchi ike!

Piss off! – Usero!; Kiero!

What type of guys do you like? – Donna taipu (no otoko) ga suki?

What are you into? – Nani ga suki?; Nani ga konomi?

I'm into... – ...ga suki; ...ga shumi.

I'm not into...; I don't like... – ...wa sukijanai; ...wa shumijanai.
  older men – Toshiue no otoko
  younger men – Toshishita no otoko
  blonde guys – Burondo no otoko; Kinpatsu no otoko
  guys with brown hair – Chairoi kami no otoko
  guys with dark hair – Kurokami no otoko
  red heads – Akage no otoko
  guys with short hair – Tanpatsu no otoko; Shōto (hea) no otoko
  guys with long hair – Rongu (hea) no otoko
  hunky guys; well-built guys – Ii karada shiteru otoko; Matcho
  thin guys – Hosomi no otoko; Yaseta otoko
  chubby guys – Potchari shita otoko
  tall guys – Senotakai otoko
  short guys – Senohikui otoko
  guys with dark eyes – Kuro me no otoko
  guys with blue eyes – Aoi me no otoko
  denim – Denimu (o kiteru otoko *-guys who wear denim*)
  leather – Rezā (o kiteru otoko *-guys who wear leather*)
  rubber – Gomu sei no fuku
  dildos – Baibu; Harigata; Dirudo

water sports – Hōnyō
fisting – Fisuto fakku
threesomes – Sanpii
cross-dressing – Josō suru no
piercing – Piasu o suru no
tattoos – Irezumi
boots – Būtsu (o haiteru otoko - *guys who wear boots*)
uniforms – Seifuku (o kiteru otoko - *guys who wear uniforms*)
brown; scat – Sukatoro
bondage – Nawa(shibari); Bondēji

Is there somewhere quieter we can go? – Doko ka shizuka na basho wa aru?

Is there somewhere more private we can go? – Futari kiri ni nareru basho wa aru?

Do you want to come to my place? – Watashi/Boku no tokoro ni konai?

Yes. – Hai

I'm sorry, I can't. – Gomen, ikenai.

Can we meet again? – Mata aeru?

When? – Itsu?

Would you like to meet me...? – ...aitai?
   this evening – Konban
   tomorrow – Ashita/Asu
   tomorrow morning – Ashita no asa
   tomorrow afternoon – Ashita no hiru; Ashita no gogo
   tomorrow night – Ashita no yoru
   on Monday – Getsuyōbi ni
   on Tuesday – Kayōbi ni
   on Wednesday – Suiyōbi ni
   on Thursday – Mokuyōbi ni
   on Friday – Kinyōbi ni
   on Saturday – Doyōbi ni
   on Sunday – Nichiyōbi ni

At what time? – Nanji ni?

At ... o'clock – ...ji (ni).

Where? – Doko de?
   here – koko de
   at my hotel – watashi/boku no hoteru de
   at my flat [UK]; apartment [US] – watashi/boku no apāto de
   at my house – watashi/boku no ie de
   at my friend's place – watashi/boku no tomodachi no tokoro de
   at your place – kimi no tokoro de

Can I have your phone number? – Denwa bangō kureru?

Can I have your address? – Jūsho kureru?

Bye! – Bai bai!

Goodbye. – Sayōnara.

See you again! – Matane!

At his place/your place – Kare no ie de/Jibun no ie de

Would you like some...? – ...hoshii?
  coffee – Kōhii
  tea – Kōcha; O-cha *(Japanese green tea)*
  wine – Wain
  orange juice – Orenji jūsu

Would you like something to eat? – Nanika tabemono hoshii?

Are you hungry/thirsty? – Onaka suiteru?/Nodo kawaita?

Are you cold/too hot? – Samui?/Atsui?

Do you want to watch T.V./a video? – Terebi/Bideo mitai?

Would you like to listen to some music? – Nanika ongaku kikitai?

What kind of music do you like? – Donna ongaku ga suki?
  classical – kurashikku
  opera – opera
  jazz – jazu
  rock – rokku
  pop – poppu
  folk – fōku
  traditional – dentōteki na ongaku *(traditional Japanese music)*; hōgaku *(any Japanese music)*

Can I kiss you? – Kisu shitemoii?

Would you like...? – ...shitehoshii? *(informal)*; ...shitehoshiidesuka? *(formal)*
  a massage – Massāji
  a blow job – Ferachio; Shakuhachi

What do you like doing? – Nani suru no ga suki?

I like... – ...ga suki.

I don't like... – ...wa sukijanai.

Do you like...? – ...ga suki? *(informal)*; ...ga sukidesuka? *(formal)*
  kissing – Kisu suru no
  cuddling – Dakiau no
  fucking – Ireru no; Anaru (sekkusu) suru no; Fakku suru no
  being fucked – Irareru no; Yarareru no; Bakku
  sucking – Sū no; Shakuhachi suru no
  being sucked – Suwareru no; Shakuhachi sareru no
  wanking; jerking off [US] – Senzuri suru no; Shigoku no; Masu o kaku no
  mutual masturbation – Issho ni shigoku no; Issho ni masu o kaku no
  licking – Nameru no; Shaburu no
  stroking – Naderu no
  rubbing – Karada o suriawaseru no
  spanking – Shiri o tataku no; Shiri o hippataku no
  being spanked – Shiri o tatakareru no; Shiri o hippatakareru no
  cross-dressing – Josō suru no
  shaving – Kezori suru no; Ke o soru no
  fisting – Fisuto fakku suru no
  rimming – Ketsu no ana o nameru no

Are you...? – Kimi...? *(informal)*; Kimi...(desuka)? *(formal)*;

I am ... - Boku/Watashi ...
  experienced – keiken ga ōi
  inexperienced – keiken ga sukunai; keiken ga amari nai

I like to be... – ...ga suki.
  active – Tachi
  passive – Neko; Ukemi

Shall we go to the bedroom/bathroom? – Beddo/Ofuro ni ikōka?

Have you got any...? – ...aru?; ...motteru?
  condoms; rubbers [US] – Kondōmu
  toys – Seigu; Tōi
  lube; lubricant – Zerii
  poppers – Rasshu

Are you into safer sex? – Sēfu sekkusu shiteru.

I'm only into safer sex. – Sēfu sekkusu shika shinai yo.

I'm HIV-positive. – Boku eichiaibii yōsei.

Are you HIV-positive? – Kimi eichiaibii yōsei?

Would you like a shower (with me)? – (Boku/Watashi to) shawā abitai?

Take off your...! – ... o nuide!; ...o totte!

Can I take off your...? – (Kimi no)... o nugashite ii?
  clothes – Fuku
  shirt – Shatsu
  trousers; pants [US] – Zubon
  socks – Sokkusu; Kutsushita
  briefs; underpants; shorts [US] – Buriifu; Pantsu; Torankusu

Lie down! – Nete!; Yokoni natte!

Bend over! – Kagande!

Sit down! – Suwatte!

You're really nice. – (Kimi) hontō ni suteki.

I like your... – Kimi no...ga suki.

Can I kiss your...? – (Kimi no)... ni kisu shitemo ii?

Can I suck your...? – (Kimi no)...o sutte ii?

Can I touch your...? – (Kimi no)...ni sawatte ii?

Can I feel your...? – (Kimi no)...o sawattemo ii?
  cock – mono *(also means 'thing')* ; ichimotsu *(also means 'thing')* ; penisu; mara; sao; nikubō; dankon; chinchin; chinpo
  balls – tama; kintama
  bum – ketsu; shiri; oshiri
  body – karada
  figure – karada no sen; karada tsuki
  nipples – chikubi
  (hairy) chest – (kebukai) mune
  legs – ashi
  toe – ashi no oyayubi; tsumasaki

That feels good! – Ii kimochi!

That's great! – Sugoku ii!
That's wonderful ! – Sugoi!
That's really good! – Sugoku ii!; Saikō!
Do that again! – Mōikkai sore shite!; Mōikkai sore yatte!; Motto motto!
My god, that's wonderful! – ā, sugoi!; ā, saikō!
Yes...yes... – Sō...sō...
Come on! – Motto motto!
Fuck me! – Fakku shite!; Irete!
Suck me! – Sutte!; Shakuhachi shite!; Shabutte!; Namete!
Wank me! – Shigoite!
Spank me! – Tataite!
Harder, harder! – Mottotsuyoku!
Slower, slower! – Motto yukkuri!
I'm coming...! – Mō iku!; Ikisō!
Come all over me! – Karada no ue de itte!; Karada jū ni kakete!
I don't like that! – Sore sukijanai!
Stop! – Yamete!
That hurts! – Sore itai!
Not so fast/hard! – Motto yukkuri/yasashiku!
Don't come in my mouth/arse! – Watashi (or Boku) no kuchi/naka de ikanaide!
That was wonderful. – Sugoku yokatta.
Would you like to clean yourself up? – Karada o fukitai?
Have you got any tissues/a towel? – Tissyu/Taoru aru?
Here you are! – Dōzo!; Hai!
May I use your shower? – (Kimi no) shawā tsukatte ii?
Shall we have a shower together? – Issho ni shawā abiyōka?
Can I have a towel (please)? – Taoru kureru (kudasai)?
Good night! – Oyasumi!
Sleep well! – Yoku nete ne! ; Gussuri nete ne!
I love you. – Aishiteru.
Did you sleep well? – Yoku neta?
I'll have to ask you to leave now. – Warui keredomo soro soro kaettekureru.
Can you go now please? – Kaettekureru.
I have to go now. – Mō kaeranaito.
Would you like some breakfast? – Asagohan taberu?

Can I write to you? – Tegami kaite ii?
It's been nice knowing you! – Tanoshikatta yo!
Would you like to see me again? – Mata attekureru?
Can I see you again? – Mata aeru?
Goodbye! – Bai bai!; Sayōnara!
See you again! – Matane!
Take care. – Genki de ne!

On the telephone – Denwa de

Hello! – Moshi moshi!
Can I speak with...(please)? – ...san irasshaimasuka?
Hang on... – chotto omachikudasai...; chotto mattekudasai...
...speaking! – ...desu!
It's me! – Watashi /Boku (desu)!
It's ... – Hai, ...desu.
I'm ringing you as we arranged. – Denwa surutte yakusoku shita kara.
Can we meet ...? – ...aeru?
   this evening – Konban
   at... o'clock – ...ji ni
Where? – doko de?
At... – ...de
Can you spell it? – Dōkaku no?
OK thank you! – Wakkata, arigatō!; Wakkata dōmo!
See you later! – Jāne!
He is not here! – Ima rusudesu!
Can you phone again... ? – ...mata kakenaoshite kuremasuka?
   later – Atode
   this afternoon – Kyō no hiru; Kyō no gogo
I don't understand. – Wakaranai. (*informal*) ; Wakarimasen. (*formal*)
Do you speak...? – ...hanasemasuka?
Please speak slowly. – Sumimasen, yukkuri hanashite kuremasuka.

Health – Kenkō

I need to see a doctor – Isha ni ikanakereba narimasen.
doctor – isha
surgery [UK]; doctor's office [US] – shinsatsushitsu
chemist [UK]; pharmacy – yakkyoku

I have... – (Watashi)...o motteimasu.
I have caught... – (Watashi)...ni kakarimashita.; (Watashi)...ni narimashita.
I think I have... – (Watashi)...ni kakatta to omoimasu.
Do you have something for...? – ...no kusuri arimasuka?
   gonorrhea – Rinbyō
   syphilis – Baidoku
   crabs – Kezirami
   lice – Shirami
   herpes – Herupesu
   scabies – Kaisen
I hurt here – Koko ga itai desu.
I'm bleeding – Chi ga dete imasu.
I'm itching – Kayui desu.
My throat/penis/anus hurts. – Nodo/Inkei /kōmon ga itai desu.

Services – Sābisu

Can you help me? – Sumimasen, tasukete kuremasuka?
How much is this/that? – Kore/Are ikuradesuka?
Have you got a map of...? – ...no chizu arimasuka?
the city – Machi
Can I have the number for Gay Switchboard? – Gei herupu rain no denwa bangō o oshiete moraemasuka?
Can I have the number of the AIDS helpline? – Eizu herupu rain no denwa bangō o oshiete kuremasuka?
Can you give me the name of a doctor who is experienced in AIDS/HIV-related problems? – Eichiaibii (*HIV*)/Eizu (*AIDS*) kanren no byōki ni kuwashii isha no namae o oshiete kuremasuka?
Can you give me the name of a clinic which is experienced in AIDS/HIV-related problems? – Eichiaibii (*HIV*)/Eizu (*AIDS*) kanren no byōki ni kuwashii byōin no namae o oshiete kuremasuka?
Can you give me the name of a gay-friendly doctor? – Gei ni shinsetsu na isha o shittemasuka?
Excuse me! – Sumimasen!
Where is/are...? – ...wa dokodesuka?
   the sauna – Sauna
   the cruising areas – Hattenba
   the gay bars – Gei bā
   the cottages [UK]; tea rooms [US] – Hatten toire
   the gay bookshop – Gei no honya
   the gay hotels – Gei hoteru

Contact ads – Kojin kōkoku/Tsūshinran

I am... – Watashi/Boku wa... (desu).

Some words in this list cannot take '...desu' at the end of the sentence; these exceptions are indicated in the list with an asterisk.

active – tachi
affectionate – aijōbukai
athletic – supōtsuman; takumashii
attractive – miryokuteki
bisexual – bai; baisekushauru; ryōtō (zukai)
boyish – bōisshu
caring – omoiyari ga arimasu.*
Christian – kirisutokyōto
chubby – futome; kobutori; potchari (shita); marupocha
clean – seiketsu
clean-shaven – hige ga nai
conservative – hoshuteki
considerate – kizukai no yoi
cuddly – dakishimetaku naruyō na hito
cute – kawaii
discreet – shinchō
dominant – tachi
easy-going – kiraku; tanoshii
educated – kyōyō ga arimasu.*
experienced – keiken hōfu
friendly – shitashimi yasui
gentle – yasashii
good-looking – rukkusu no yoi; hansamu
hairy – kebukai
handsome – hansamu
honest – shōjiki
horny – sekkusu zuki; seiyoku ōsei
I have a good sense of humour – Watashi/Boku wa yūmoa no sensu ga arimasu.
independent – dokuritsushin ōsei
inexperienced – keikenga sukunai *(little experience)*; mikeiken *(no experience)*
intelligent – chiteki
interesting – omoshiroi
introverted – naikōteki
lonely – sabishii; kodoku
loyal – seijitsu
married – kikon
masculine – otokorashii; otokoppoi
mature – seijuku shita
of medium build – chūniku chūzei
middle aged – chūnen; midorueiji
military – gunjin; jei kan
muscular – takumashii; matcho; gatchiri to shita
a nature lover – shizen aikōka
non-scene – gei shiin ni ikimasen*; nichōme ni ikimasen.*
a non-smoker – tabako o suimasen; non sumōkā; kin enka
older – toshiue; ani(ki) *('an older brother')*
open – Ōpun
open minded – henken ga nai

outgoing – gaikōteki; yōki; kaikatsu
passionate – jōnetsuteki
passive – neko; ukemi; anaru ukemi; anaru zuki
quiet – otonashii; monoshizuka
radical – kageki
refined – senrensarete imasu.*
reliable – shinrai seiga arimasu.*
reserved – enryobukai
romantic – romanchikku
sensitive – sensai
serious – majime; shinken
shy – uchiki; hito mishiri
sincere – seijitsu
slim – surimu
a smoker – tabako o suimasu.*
smooth – kebukaku nai
special – tokubetsu
spontaneous – shōdōteki
sporty – supōtii; supōtsuman; supōtsuzuki
straight acting – nonkeppoi
straight forward – sotchoku
a student – (dai)gakusei
submissive – jūjun; neko; ukemi
tall – chōshin; se ga takai
transsexual – nyūhāfu; seitenkansha
a university graduate – daisotsu
a virgin – bājin; dōtei
warm – atatakai
well-endowed; well-hung – pii dai; deka mara; deka chin; uma nami
well-built – taikaku no yoi; rippa na taikaku
young – wakai; yangu ('a young man'); seinen ('a young man')
younger – toshishita; otōto ('a younger brother')
youthful – wakawakashii

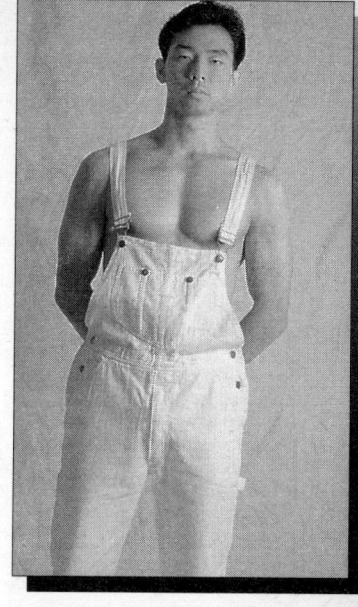

I am looking for ... – ... motomu; ... ... o sagashiteimasu.

Most Japanese contact ads express 'looking for a...guy' as 'looking for a...person' (e.g. 'an affectionate person', or 'an athletic person'). The word hito, *which means 'person' may be substituted for* otoko, *meaning 'a man'. In many cases the reference to 'a person' (no/na* hito) *is optional and is shown in the list in brackets. e.g. 'I am looking for an active guy' can be:* Tachi no hito motomu, *or just simplified to* Tachi motomu.

an active guy – Tachi (no hito)
an affectionate guy – Aijōbukai hito
an athletic guy – Supōtsuman; Takumashii hito
an attractive guy – Miryokuteki na hito
a bisexual guy – Bai (no otoko); Baisekushuaru (no otoko); Ryōtō (zukai) (no otoko)
a boyish guy – Bōisshu na hito
a caring guy – Omoiyari no aru hito
a Christian guy – Kirisutokyōto (no hito)
a chubby guy – Futome (no hito); Kobutori (na hito); Potchari (shita) hito; Marupocha (na hito)
a clean guy – Seiketsu (na hito)
a clean-shaven guy – Hige ga nai hito
a conservative guy – Hoshuteki (na hito)
a considerate guy – Kizukai no yoi hito
a cuddly guy – Dakishimetaku naruyō na hito

a cute guy – Kawaii hito; Kawaii (otoko no) ko *('a cute boy')*
a discreet guy – Shinchō (na hito)
a dominant guy – Tachi (no hito)
an easy-going guy – Kiraku na hito; Tanoshii hito
an educated guy – Kyōyō ga aru hito
an experienced guy – Keiken hōfu (na hito)
a friendly guy – Shitashimi yasui hito
a gentle guy – Yasashii hito
a good-looking guy – Rukkusu no yoi hito; Hansamu (na hito)
a hairy guy – Kebukai hito
a handsome guy – Hansamu (na hito)
an honest guy – Shōjiki na hito
a horny guy – Sekkusu zuki (na hito); Seiyoku ōsei (na hito)
a guy with a good sense of humour – Yūmoa no sensu ga aru hito
an independent guy – Dokuritsushin ōsei na hito
an inexperienced guy – Keikenga sukunai hito *(little experience)* Mikeiken (no hito) *(no experience)*
an intelligent guy – Chiteki (na hito)
an interesting guy – Omoshiroi hito
an introverted guy – Naikōteki na hito
a lonely guy – Sabishii hito; Kodoku na hito
a loyal guy – Seijitsu na hito
a married guy – Kikon (no hito)
a masculine guy – Otokorashii (hito); Otokoppoi hito
a mature guy – Seijuku shita hito
a guy of medium build – Chūniku chūzei (no hito)
a middle aged guy – Chūnen (no hito); Midorueiji (no hito)
a military guy – Gunjin (no hito); Jei kan (no hito)
a muscular guy – Takumashii hito; Matcho (na hito); Gatchiri to shita hito
a nature lover – Shizen aikōka (no hito)
a non-scene guy – Gei shiin ni ikanai hito; Nichōme ni ikanai hito
a non-smoker – Tabako o suwanai hito; Non sumōkā (no hito); Kin enka (no hito)
an older guy – Toshiue (no hito); Ani(ki) ('an older brother')
an open guy – Ōpun na hito
an open minded guy - Henken ga nai hito
an outgoing guy – Gaikōteki na hito; Yōki na hito; Kaikatsu na hito
a passionate guy – Jōnetsuteki na hito
a passive guy – Neko (no hito); Ukemi (no hito); Anaru ukemi (no hito); Anaru zuki (no hito)
a quiet guy – Otonashii hito; Monoshizuka na hito
a radical guy – Kageki na hito
a refined guy – Senrensareta hito
a reliable guy – Shinrai dekiru hito
a reserved guy – Enryobukai hito
a romantic guy – Romanchikku (na hito)
a guy of the same age – Dōnendai (no hito)
a sensitive guy – Sensai na hito
a serious guy – Majime (na hito); Shinken na hito
a shy guy – Uchiki (na hito); Hito mishiri na hito
a sincere guy – Seijitsu (na hito)
a slim guy – Surimu (na hito)
a smoker – Tabako o sū hito
a smooth guy – Kebukaku nai hito
a special guy – Tokubetsu na hito
a spontaneous guy – Shōdōteki na hito
a sporty guy – Supōtii na hito; Supōtsuman; Supōtsuzuki (na hito)

a straight acting guy – Nonkeppoi (hito)
a straight forward guy – Sotchoku na hito
a student – (Dai)gakusei
a submissive guy – Jūjun (na hito); Neko (no hito); Ukemi (no hito)
a tall guy – Chōshin (no hito); Se no takai hito
a transsexual – Nyūhāfu; Seitenkansha
a university graduate – Daisotsu (no hito)
a virgin – Bājin (no hito); Dōtei (no hito)
a warm guy – Atatakai hito
a well-endowed guy; a well-hung guy – Pii dai (no hito); Deka mara (no hito); Deka chin (no hito); Uma nami (no hito)
a well-built guy – Taikaku no yoi hito; Rippa na taikaku no hito
a young guy – Wakai hito; Yangu ('a young man'); Seinen ('a young man')
a younger guy – Toshishita (no hito); Otōto ('a younger brother")
a youthful guy – Wakawakashii hito
no effeminates. – Joseiteki fuka; Onē fuka; Joseiteki nakata okotowari; Onē okotowari.
no fats. – Futtota hito fuka; Debu fuka *(offensive)*; Futtota hito okotowari; Debu okotowari. *(offensive)*
...welcome – ...kangei
for friendship – Tomodachi motomu; Dachikō motomu.
for a relationship – Koibito motomu.
for sex – Sekkusu motomu.
...only – ... (to shite) nomi.
I have... – ...desu.
  blue eyes – Aoi me
  brown eyes – Chairo no me; Kuro me *(very dark brown)*
  green eyes – Midori no me
  grey eyes – Haiiro no me
  blonde hair – Burondo; Kinpatsu
  brown hair – Chairoi kami
  black hair – Kuroi kami
  red hair – Akage
  grey hair – Haiiro no kami
  dark hair – Kurokami
  short hair – Tanpatsu; Shōto (hea); Supōtsukari *(very short hair)*
  long hair – Rongu (hea)

I have a beard. – Agohige ga arimasu.

I have a moustache. – Kuchihige ga arimasu.

I'm bald. – Hage te imasu.

Expressions – Hyōgen

My God! – Ō!; Wa!

Fantastic! – Subarashii!; Suteki!

I'm sorry. – Sumimasen *(formal)*; Gomen. *(informal)*

Excuse me! – Sumimasen!; Shitsurei!

Get fucked! – Damare!; Kusottare!

Fuck off! – Usero!

Shit! – Kuso!; Chikushō!; Che!

Darling! – Anata!; Omae!
My dear! – Anata!; Omae!
Honey! – Anata!
Oh dear! – Ā!; Oya!
How wonderful! – Sugoi!; Suteki!; Subarashii!
How awful! – Kimochi warui!; Hidoi!
He's a friend of Dorothy. – Kare wa kotchino hito; Kare wa onakama.
As camp as knickers. – Sugoi onē; (Sugoi) ōgosho.
Wow! – Wa!; Ō!

Other useful vocabulary – Hosoku go

Yes – Hai
No – Iie
I am... – Watashi/Boku wa...(desu).
he is... – Kare wa...(desu).
you are.... – Kimi wa...(desu) *(informal)*; Anata wa...(desu) (formal); *[person's name]* wa...(desu).
my friend is... – Watashi/Boku no tomodachi wa...(desu).
my friends are... – Watashi/Boku no tomodachi wa...(desu).
my boyfriend is... – Watashi /Boku no kare wa...(desu); Watashi /Boku no kareshi wa...(desu).
adult – adaruto
AIDS – Eizu
bent [UK]; homo [US] – homoppoi (*adj*); hentai (*adj*)
bisexual – bai; baisekushuaru; ryōtō (zukai)
a bitch – kuso onna *(usually to a woman)*; bitchi
to bitch – kageguchi o iu; ijiwaru o suru
bitchy – ijiwaru
body-building – bodii biru
butch – otokoppoi; otoko mitai (*to a woman*)
camp – okamappoi; joseiteki
to chat someone up – kudoku
to be 'in the closet' – kakuregei; gei de arukoto o kakusu
come; cum; spunk – zāmen; seieki; superuma
to come – iku
to 'come out' – kamu auto; jibun ga gei de arukoto o ukeireru
a cow – yana onna

to cruise – hatten suru

drag – josō

drag shows – josō shō

a dyke; a lesbo [US] – yuri

a butch dyke – rezu matcho; otokoyaku no rezu; otokoppoi rezu

erect – tatsu; katakunaru

an erection; a hard-on – bokki

a fag hag – okoge

female – josei

french-kissing – diipu kisu

a fuck – fakku; anaru (sekkusu)

gay – gei; homo; bara; dōseiaisha *(homosexual - noun)*

the gay scene – gei shiin

a girl – onna; anoko

a guy – otoko; yatsu; aitsu

the leather scene – rezā shiin

a lesbian – rezu; rezubian

male – dansei

men only – dansei nomi

the nightclub – (naito) kurabu

the nudist beach – nūdisuto biichi

to pick someone up – hikkakeru

to be pissed off with someone – mukatsuku; unzari suru

a poof; a faggot [US] – okama; homo (yarō); kagema

a queen – okama; onē

queer – gei *(adj & noun)*; homo *(adj & noun)*; kama *(adj & noun)*; okamappoi *(adj)*; homoppoi *(adj)*; onakama *(noun)*

queer-bashing – gei-basshingu

a rent boy – urisen

SM (sadomasochism) – esuemu; sado-mazo

skinheads – sukinheddo

a slut – daresen *(to a man)*; shirigaru *(to a woman)*; yariman *(both sexes)*; baita

straight – nonke; sutorēto

a tart – hade; kebai

a transvestite – josō; oyama

a wank – masu; masutābēshon; onanii; senzuri

women only – josei nomi
one ichi
two – ni
three – san
four – yon; shi
five – go
six –roku
seven – nana; shichi
eight – hachi
nine – ku/kyū
ten – jū
eleven – jūichi
twelve – jūni
thirteen – jūsan
fourteen – jūyon; jūshi
fifteen –jūgo
sixteen – jūroku
seventeen – jūnana; jūshichi
eighteen – jūhachi
nineteen – jūku; jūkyū
twenty – nijū
twenty one – nijūichi
twenty two – nijūni
thirty – sanjū
forty – yonjū
fifty – gojū
sixty – rokujū
seventy – nanajū; shichijū
eighty – hachijū
ninety – kyūjū
one hundred – hyaku
one thousand – sen
ten thousand – ichiman

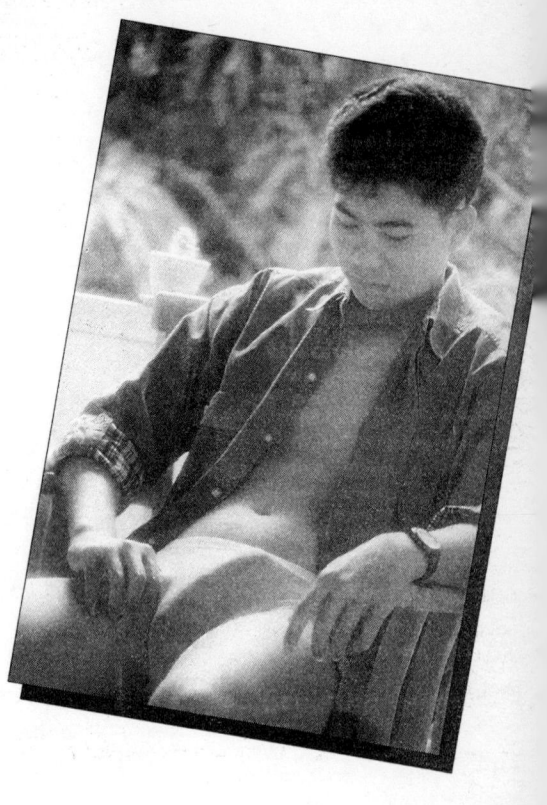

Talking safer sex!

In a sauna – Sauna de

Hello, I'm James. I'm Australian.
Konnichiwa, watashi wa Jēmusu desu. Ōsutorariajin desu

I'm Minoru.
Watashi wa Minoru desu.

Do you know where I can find a gay sauna?
Gei sauna wa doko ni aruka shitteimasuka?

Mmm, I know one. I'll show you where it is.
Un, hitotsu shitteimasu. Annai shimashō.

    (... on the way ...
    ...tochū de...)

I've seen a lot of bath houses and saunas here in Japan.
Watashi wa nihon de takusan no sentō to sauna o mikakemashita.

Yes, you have to be very careful if you go into one. Most of them are not gay. You have to be very discreet.
Hai, soko ni ittara chūishite kudasai. Hotondo wa gei de wa nai no de shinchō ni kōdō shite kudasai.

    (...later...
    ...atode...)

Is this a gay sauna?
Kore wa gei sauna desuka?

Yes, this one is.
Hai, sō desu.

Do they allow foreigners inside this sauna?
Gaikokujin demo hairemasuka?

Yes.
Hai.

How much is it?
Ikura desuka?

2000 Yen.
Nisen en desu.

You need to put your shoes in this locker first...
Kutsu o kono rokkā ni irete kudasai...

Where is the shower room?
Shawā wa doko desuka?

Next to the sauna.
Sauna no yoko desu.

It's a big place. Have you been here before?
Hiroi desu ne! Izen ni kitakoto ga arimasuka?

Yes. I thought this was the best one to come to. In most saunas they don't let foreigners in. They are scared it will increase the spread of AIDS in Japan.
Hai, watashi wa koko ga ichiban ii to omoimasu. Hotondo no sauna wa gaikokujin wa irete kuremasen. Karera wa eizu ga nihon ni hirogaru no o osoreteimasu.

Do they show gay movies in here?
Koko de wa gei no eiga o hōei shiteimasuka?

Let's have a look around!
Sā, sokora o mitekimashō.

> (... a bit later ...
> ...sukoshi atode...)

Would you like to go to a room?
Koshitsu e ikimasenka?

OK!
Ii desu yo!

Do they have condoms and lube here?
Koko ni kondōmu to zerii wa oiteimasuka?

Yes, I'll get some... just wait...
Hai, morattekimasu... Sukoshi matte kudasai...

Here... we can take this room.
Sā...kono koshitsu o tsukaimashō.

Let me roll the condom on your cock.
Kondōmu o kabusemashō.

You do that very well!
Totemo umai desu ne!

Do you like sucking? Fucking?
Shakuhachi soretomo irerareru no ga sukidesuka?

Fuck me!
Irete!

Suck me! Suck my dick!
Sutte! Shakuhachi shite!

You were great!
Totemo yokatta!

Let's have a shower together.
Issho ni shawā o abimashō.

Thank you. I hope to see you again. Bye!
Arigatō! Mata oaishitai desu. Sayōnara!

Bye!
Sayōnara!

OG

Oriental Guys

More than just a magazine.
It's a lifestyle

The world's Premier and luxurious quarterly publication on Asia's most beautiful men. Filled with breathtaking pictorial spreads, features, fiction, travel, pen-pals and much more!

photographer: Luis Supangco

photographer: Ma-Ten

Order the latest OG issues from:
International Wavelength Inc. 2215-R Market St#829, San Francisco, CA 94114
Tel: (415) 864-6500, Fax: (415) 864-6615, e - mail: intwave@netcom.com

The publisher wishes to thank Prowler Press Limited for use of the photographs in this book. Photographer credits and the title of the Prowler Press magazine in which each photo has appeared follow:

cover photo	**LPI (*Euroboy*)**
page 1 by	**Derek Powers (*Euroboy*)**
page 2 by	**Priapic (*Euroboy*)**
page 14 by	**Boyproof Studio (*Euroboy*)**
page 20 by	**LPI (*Euroboy*)**
page 28 by	**Champion (*Euroboy*)**
page 32 by	**Pedro Usabiaga (*Hunk*)**
page 36 by	**Champion (*Euroboy*)**
page 40 by	**Michael Taubenheim (*Hunk*)**
page 52 by	**Priapic (*Euroboy*)**
page 55 by	**Roma Studio (*Euroboy*)**
page 56 by	**Pedro Usabiaga (*Euroboy*)**
page 62 by	**GPH (*Euroboy*)**
page 70 by	**Pedro Usabiaga (*Euroboy*)**
page 72 by	**LPI (*Euroboy*)**
page 76 by	**Derek Powers (*Euroboy*)**
page 90 by	**Brad Posey (*Euroboy*)**
page 93 by	**Champion (*Euroboy*)**
page 98 by	**GPH (*Euroboy*)**
page 108 by	**Junior Studio (*Prowl*)**
page 112 by	**Boyproof Studio (*Euroboy*)**
page 114 by	**Eric Basior (*Steam*)**
cover photo	**LPI (*Euroboy*)**

Other photos by Prowler Press photographers, except for those of Japanese models which are courtesy of *OG* magazine.

Safer Sexy is a new and revolutionary guide to gay safer sex and well-being.

'Erotic, comprehensive and common-sensical'
Sir Ian McKellen

'This book will save lives'
Holly Johnson

Sumptuously and explicitly illustrated, *SAFER SEXY* demonstrates how to have exciting and satisfying gay sex, safely.

112 pages, 96 colour photographs

Don't let anything come between you and him...

EXCEPT RUBBER!

Written and devised by **Peter Tatchell**.

Photographs by **Robert Taylor**.

Available from the Cassell Sexual Politics list

Sponsored by Ivan Massow Associates.

Endorsed by:

Gay Men Fighting AIDS